W9-BSU-061

The Summer of

NICOLE LEA HELGET

BOREALIS
BOOKS

The Summer of Ordinary Ways

For my sisters

For Isabella, Mitchell, and Phillip

The Summer of Ordinary Ways

Let nothing cruel stir in my blood again.
PAUL ZIMMER, "Confession, Curse and Prayer"

The Summer of Ordinary Ways

Stain You Red

(SUMMER 1983)

Dad crouched, slack knees to his chest, in front of the barn wall with his mitt and told me to pitch him a few. He punched a fist into his glove, pointed two fingers down, then opened his hand, wiped the sign away, and pointed just one finger down. A fastball.

"Put her right here," he said.

He had set down a beer can in front of him, home plate, and positioned a wooden bat in Annie Jo's hands, the fading name, *William Helget*, burned on the barrel of it. He pointed at a spot in the grass where she should stand and told her not to move, not to swing, and to hold the bat high. It almost toppled her.

"Choke up," he said.

I wound into a pitch and released the ball to him with all the force my fifty-pound frame could gather. The ball slapped his glove.

"Nice one."

He tossed it back in an easy way. I threw a few more. Strikes. Then a pitch missed, and flew up and outside the strike zone I'd mind-outlined above the beer can, bending in on Annie Jo's body, but Dad caught it without compromising his stance, pulled it quick into the center of him.

"That's how you get the strikes called. The umps look to where the ball sits when they make the calls. It's the catcher's job to pull 'em in."

I know, Dad.

I know, too, Dad, Annie Jo said. I do, Dad, I know.

"You just hold that bat up, Annie-Goat. Nice and high so Colie doesn't hit your elbows. She's wild sometimes."

I threw again. Annie Jo swung and foul-tipped the ball back into a barn window.

"Goddamn it," Dad said. "I told you not to swing." He stood, cast down his glove, and grabbed the bat from Annie Jo, who cowered beneath him. She was four.

He pointed at the window with the bat. "Do you know how many fucking flies are going to get in there? Do you? Put this shit away. Hurry up now. And quit your goddamned crying. I can't stand it. It goes right through me."

He lobbed the bat at her feet. She knew not to move.

"Colie, you pick up that glass there and dig in the wood pile. Find a piece of plywood to cover that window. Fuck. Goddamn it. Useless, completely useless."

He turned from us and headed for the barn.

Dad was thirty-one. He was tall and lean with Bohemian,

colored dark with Sioux Indian from his mother Alvina's side—a bunch of lost gypsies and buffalo eaters, he called them. His father, Leon Helget, was thick with German blood and passed on his tumbling speech and throaty voice to his seven sons, including Dad, who was just one up from the bottom, but bossy as an oldest child or an Indian chief. And that's the name Dad's brothers gave him—Chief. Dad's long legs bowed at the knees from his years crouching behind home plate and against a cow's belly for the milking. He walked with his hands on his hips like he was operating those loose legs from there.

Dad said three major league teams scouted him his senior year of high school at Sleepy Eye St. Mary's. In 1972, two Boston Red Sox agents, sipping coffee and eating slices of schmeirkuchen, pushed a creased stack of papers across Grandma's kitchen table at Dad. He signed to a Triple A contract while Grandpa, who mostly spoke Low German, sat silent and crossed his arms tight against his overalls. Grandpa had a farm place and land ready for Dad, and he didn't see the sense of his son running all over God's creation when there were perfectly good ballparks around here. But Grandma had warned him to keep his mouth shut and told him that baseball was Dad's chance.

You're an old fool, Grandma said, and I don't like that goat language in this house. Goat-herders, that's where you come from.

Goddamn gypsy, Grandpa spat.

Dad signed the contract and prepared to leave the following winter for spring training. He said no to the Cincinnati Reds and the Minnesota Twins and proposed to his girlfriend, Marie, after she graduated from high school, and in their *Sleepy Eye Herald Dispatch* wedding announcement it said, *Marie Haala was Homecoming Queen at Sleepy Eye St. Mary's and William Helget catches for the Boston Red Sox organization, which is currently in spring training in Winter Haven, Florida. The couple will reside there.*

Dad and Mom lived in Winter Haven while Dad practiced, played, and traveled with the team. Mom hated the heat and the cockroaches and the wives of the other players. A year into their marriage and Dad's baseball career, the doctors induced a labor and delivered Mom of a dead baby, which they whisked quickly away. Mom never thought to ask the sex of it, though Dad always said it was a son and his name would have been Nicholas because he liked the way "Nick" sounded over the loud speaker of a ball field. Nick Helget.

When she became pregnant with me, Mom insisted she be near her family in Minnesota. Grandpa Helget readied the farm place, and Mom moved onto it and waited for Dad. She had me in March of 1976, and Dad made it to my birth but left the next day to go back to spring training. Grandma Helget said wives should be with their husbands, said the farm place could wait. She packed up Mom and me and drove us back to Florida, back to the heat and the cockroaches and the other player's wives, and stayed with us until we were settled.

. . .

The Red Sox released Dad in 1977. They said he couldn't hit, though they liked that he was a switcher. They said his knees were bound to give soon. They patted him on the back and said he called good pitches, said they liked the way he signaled the outfielders, too. They liked how he knew which way the ball was going if the batter got a hold of it. Amazing. You've got good instinct for baseball, son. You should go home and coach your little girl's softball team when the time comes. You can turn in your uniform and keys at the field house. Here's your commemorative bat. Isn't that nice? It's got your name burned in it. Cost the outfit a buck or two. Keep the cap and send us your new address, why don't you. Keep in touch.

When each of their seven sons married, Grandpa and Grandma Helget gave the new couple a homestead with a house and outbuildings for livestock, grain, and machinery, eighty acres of tillable land for corn and soybeans, twenty cows, a bull, and a pickup. After the Red Sox let Dad go, he came home to Minnesota to farm. Mom settled in. Dad woke in the dark mornings to the bellowing of cows playing chords in his ears. He knew the call of each one. Sometimes, Mom's noises from boiling water to heat the bottles for the five daughters that tagged after me roused Dad from his dreams of nick-of-time throw-outs at second and of blocking home plate from a barreling Pete Rose, who would never jar the ball loose from him the way he did from Ray Fosse in the 1970 All-Star game. Put it in your nut cup if you have to, goddamn it, but don't let 'em get the ball loose, he'd say to Fosse in those sleepy imaginings. He told Mom about the dreams over breakfast after the milking, after he romanced them and the game in his mind for hours in the barn with the cows, while pitching straw and cleaning gutters and salving infected teats and grinding corn and throwing hay bales down from the loft and spraying for the flies that bred, maggoted, morphed, and seemed to emerge from the very air in the barn, and while moving from cow to cow pumping milk from the beasts that trapped him in that place with their never-ending needs. Feeding, cleaning, doctoring, milking. A woman's job, really, he'd say of it, and Mom would look at him, set down the fry pan or a drooling baby, and say he had to stop drinking brandy because that's when the dreams came racing and forced him fidgety and violent in his sleep, unsatisfied. You've got to be satisfied with what you've got, William. Thank God for it.

On Sundays, Dad caught for Stark, an amateur baseball team that played in the middle of a field, where lost baseballs, walloped over center field by local boys, became fertilizer for the worming roots of corn and soybeans. The red stitches wore away and surrendered the cow-hide leather, cotton string, wool winding, rubber covers, and cork centers to the black soil. Mom and my sisters and I watched the game from the grandstands with the other wives and children. Mom swapped recipes for jello salads and hot dish. I kept book. Dad wanted all the statistics. Errors. Sacrifices. Stolen bases.

Runs batted in. Number of pitches thrown per inning. All of it. He went through the book at night after the evening milking and punched numbers into a calculator and scratched stats and strategies on the backs of envelopes, on our homework, in the white space of newspapers. He relived the game. "It's 90 percent mental, Colie. The game. It's 90 percent mental and 10 percent physical," he'd say.

I know, Dad, but you're writing on my homework.

Dad gripped the chain fence behind me and called instructions. My thighs and hamstrings blazed with the strain of squatting under the weight of my body, the mask, the chest protector, and the leg guards. I had been holding out my arm receiving pitches into my catcher's mitt for an hour and we were only in the fourth inning. The Sleepy Eye St. Mary's varsity softball team pulled me up from B-squad in ninth grade to catch for Julie Schulmacher, who was fast, but wild. She was all over the place and threw more pitches per batter than I had ever seen.

Once Coach pulled me up there to catch, Dad came to all our practices and games. The older girls would toss sunflower seeds at him and grab for his cap. Jessie Heiderschiet, our senior right fielder, asked Dad about his stops at Meyer's Bar in Sleepy Eye, where her mom worked, and told the team about the time she had to give him a ride home because he was too drunk on Five Star to drive. They shushed and half-smiled when I came in earshot, but I knew all of it already and had heard other stories besides. Coach finally asked him to stop coming to practice, said he was a distraction. But Dad still stood behind home plate for every game I caught and called me back after each inning for pointers.

"Pull 'em in, Colie. Some of those are close. If you'd get 'em into you quicker, the ump would give her some of those outside ones," he said.

Shit, Dad. She's everywhere. She's throwing like a million pitches an inning, and I'm chasing all the fouls because she won't get off the mound. I'm tired, and I'm on deck. I gotta get this stuff off.

"Well, pull it together. You look like hell back here, for Christ's sakes. It's a goddamned embarrassment."

I quit as catcher after that game even though it meant I went back to B-squad.

After I quit catching, Dad never came to another softball game. Not mine, or Annie Jo's, or Natty's, or Lila's, or Dakota's, or Mia's. Not one.

Humidity fogged the barn. Straw dust stuck in my hair and under my arms in a sweaty film that attracted the flies, the biting kind with black bodies and iridescent green heads. It was time to wean the calf from the cow. Newborn calves and their mothers settle together in the nursing pen of the barn for a few days after the birth so the calf can nurse from its mother and ingest antibodies that saturate the thin milk, colostrum, in those few days. When the cow's marketable milk lets down later, the calf is pulled from its mother and bottle-fed a supplement. The cow returns to the milking population. Her rich product improves the quality of the whole supply.

This cow, Big Jenny, just days before a heifer—a cow who had never birthed—stood like granite in front of her calf in the nursing pen. I had been spreading protein pellets on the feed for the cows locked in their milking stanchions, the cows who had birthed, weaned, and separated from their calves before and who were used to milking.

Dad called me over.

He pushed against Big Jenny's haunch with his upper arm and shoulder. The calf danced under its mother and around her legs.

"Pull that calf away now, Colie. I've got the rope around his neck. Just pull it a bit. He'll come."

The calf stamped backwards against my pulling. I didn't want to hurt him, so I didn't tug hard.

"Try luring him with the bottle."

He's not coming, Dad. Can't he just stay with his mom?

Dad pushed on the cow's backside. "Come on now, bossy. You're done with this business. No more. You've got to get back with the girls. He'll be fine here. Nothing to worry about."

Big Jenny didn't go.

"Get me that pitchfork there."

I believed he meant just to tap her as I'd seen him do before. A little poke to keep the herd moving in and out of the barn, like a parent placing a soft swat on the bottom of a lagging child. I handed him the pitchfork.

He used the curved end of the prongs to thump her behind a few times. The fork dropped against the black fur and sent flies up into the barn air like dust particles released from the rugs Mom beat on the clothesline.

"Come on, now. Get." He hit her again. Her flank muscles twitched, sending ripples into the fat and fur along her belly.

"Move." He pushed her again with his shoulder. He heaved himself against her loin, but still she wouldn't budge. She flicked flies off her ears and swatted ones on her back with her tail. Dad grabbed the calf by the rope and pulled him off into the corner, tied him to a post. Big Jenny followed and sniffed her calf between his legs.

"You're coming out of here. I've had enough of this. We don't have time for this shit. Colie, come stand between them."

I did, though I was scared of Big Jenny's girth and her mood. I had been kicked before, and a scar, tanless and half-moon shaped, stretched the skin on my ankle.

A halogen bulb hung from a rusty chain, hovered above the cow's head. He picked up the pitchfork again and started swinging at the cow's backside. Once. Twice. The whiff of the swings sent the lone bulb waving. Slap, Slap, like my pitches hitting Dad's glove. Again and again, but she still wouldn't leave the calf.

"Goddamn it." Dad slammed the pitchfork into the hay at the cow's hoof. It punched through the straw and rang against the floor, metal against concrete, and when it bounced back, Dad hit there again.

He got a feel for the rebounding effect and moved all around Big Jenny stabbing near her hooves. The cow lifted her legs, contracted her muscles, and puffed from her nostrils. Saliva hit my arm. She stayed at her calf, though. And I stood between the two. There was a sort of comedy then with Dad poking around the straw, Big Jenny lazily swatting flies, the calf pushing my bottom to reach its mother, and me, stifling nervous giggles.

Dad moved next to me, planted his feet, and lifted the pitchfork. He stabbed Big Jenny in the nose and cracked metal against her bones. A sound snapped the thick air.

Like eggs dropped on the wooden floor of the chicken coop. Or metal bats whacking leather-covered baseballs. There was something of a wooden ruler slapping naughty palms. Something of thunder breaking against the sky. Only more primal, more rooted. I recognized it immediately. For eight years it drummed under my feet and echoed in my breath. It was the sound of girls splitting wish-bones, of Mom dividing chicken breasts, and of shovels crushing black rats breeding in the granary. It was the sound of field stones hitting the loader bucket or hay wagon or rock box. It was the sound of a cottonwood tree, lifted from the lawn, twisted, and sailed into the drying bin by a tornado, the sound of the collision and explosion of wood and metal and the rush of millions of soybean grains winding in a golden vein, breaking through the gape, and flying off into a gray heaven. It was the sound of Adam's rib breaking to build Eve. It was bone.

. . .

He hesitated. Dad brought the pitchfork back and tapped at the air, gaining inches and conviction each time. Years of carrying, loading, throwing, pushing, and pulling the elements of that farm had fashioned his back and arms into rolling furrows and knolls. His bottom lip folded over his top and touched the coarse hairs of his moustache. Maybe in that pause, he thought about caring for these animals all his life, for that one especially. He had pulled that calf from Big Jenny three days before. He reached into her body, sought two front hooves delicate as soil clumps, and drew them from her womb in a flood of amniotic fluid. The calf emerged and landed against Dad's body, felt the warmth of his bare chest and the strength of his arms. The calf heard the bass of Dad's voice when he said to his daughters, sitting quietly on a straw bale, "Well, there he is. A keeper, I guess."

But maybe he didn't think of this. Maybe he only thought about how dumb and tired and indifferent this cow was, how she defied him. Dad pierced her again, along the cheek and under her eye and harder this time. She threw up her back legs and bawled against the assault. He let down a rage on her neck. This blow stuck into her fur, through her skin, and into the muscle. It was a clumsy strike. He struggled to release the pitchfork from her. Blood pooled in the four holes, shaped droplets that pulled crimson threads down her white fur, and finally fell to the floor. The routes established, her neck freed life in steady pulses.

. . .

Measure it against something. A wood splinter, a thumb tack, a vaccination, an imbedded nail. Who can say what sensations an animal suffers? How can it feel to be impaled with the dull, dirty prongs of a pitchfork? How far does the skin dent before it yields finally and breaks under the pressure? Does Jesus weep for this animal the way Sister Gertrude, your religion teacher, said He wept for the ants you crushed at recess while you danced around their mounds and kicked up your skirt before God and everybody and offended Jesus with your shamelessness? Does He weep because you stand there and watch your dad bring the pitchfork to the poor creature again and again and you don't remind your dad that he's a Christian, a Catholic? Does Jesus weep because you want to push that calf, the one whose wet breath pants on your thighs, in front of you and hide in the shadow of his body quivering with fear, and hunger, and newness?

And the fork goes in again. Slow it. Consider the four points invading vessels, tendons, and muscle and leaving rust and manure and straw. And what of the nerves? Do they buzz with consciousness? What messages do they send to the beast's brain? Do they bring shock and resistance against the pain? Or do they simply spring back and forth trying to bridge the connection on the other side of the puncture wounds and send down the hurt that keeps her conscious, the hurt that reminds her animal mind to run or escape or protect herself? Where are her instincts? Or is that what keeps her here? She's a mother. Just days a mother. Her insides still churn, returning to their proper place. The organs are shifting as the pitchfork invades them, the spikes stop their progress. She'll die with her lungs not quite in the right place, her stomachs still pressed small, her intestines entwined, her heart pushed too far into her throat. Her organs weren't ready. They were still feeling for the baby that had rooted and grown there and were adjusting, trying to remember their place in the void.

Consider the man who does this. A man who can be so lovely sometimes that you and your sisters collect under the wonder of him and take turns clinging to his legs while he strides in the lawn. A man who fries eggs and potatoes in an iron skillet for his wife because she loves them while she watches the ten o'clock news and who won't be upset when the scent draws you from your beds and who will fry more potatoes and eggs and then send you back to bed with the treat settling in your stomachs. A man who will quarter, core, and salt green apples until your eyes pucker with the brack and sour. A man who hits you pop flies as high as the barn turret. A man who teaches you to change a tire, drive a stick shift, change oil, test the moisture of soybeans, shoot a rifle, drink beer, and throw like a boy. A man who comes home from bowling loaded with cigarette smoke and brandy and trips over your bodies, sleeping on the living room floor because of the heat, and falls and laughs and says, Colie. Annie-Goat. Natty. What are you doing down here? Did the devil deliver you? I'm thinking about buying a horse. Would you like a horse? And of course you would and you fall back to sleep relieved but knowing that there will be no horse and the morning will be quiet and you will have to play outside all day while he recovers and you will help your mom milk the loaded cows so that the mastitis doesn't infect the herd while your dad fumes against his head, the ache and the thoughts. The straw bales, heavy and cumbersome, demand the strength of two of you and the five-gallon pails can only be filled halfway with feed because you're small, you Helget girls, and thin. But your muscles tone like sad smiles on your arms because of days like this and you will bed and feed the cows as well as anyone's sons. He has something terrible waking in him, your mother whispers into the phone. The priest will come and talk to your dad and tell him to pray for healing and your dad will tell the priest to get the fuck off his property. Your mom will have a black eye once for singing in the car. Shut up, he'll say, and strike her in the face. Another time, he'll come home and drag her out of bed by the hair and say, Make me some bacon and eggs, and she will but she won't fry the eggs in the bacon grease the way he likes them and he'll take the fry pan off the burner and throw it at her and scorch a grease burn the size of a softball on her arm and splatter fire marks like stars down it to her hand and she will call to you, Come and help me. Hurry, please. Splash water on my hand. My God. My hand. Oh Jesus. Oh shit. It burns. It burns. Colder water. Get some ice. And the hand spots with red blisters and you will say, But Mom the skin is *peeling* from your arm. And it is peeling. Her skin falls in leaves from her arm. It singes back, curls, and releases. Just like leaves or scales or feathers or potato peelings. Oh Mom. Your arm.

Look at your arm. I can't feel that, she'll say. And it's true. She can't feel it because it's burned past the nerves, down three degrees of medical terminology. The nerves are dead and thank God for it. Put some butter on it, your dad will say before he's gone again out the door and off to town. And then the grandparents will come and take your mom to the emergency room and she'll stay there for days and she'll go back often. The doctors will take pieces from her thigh and patch them on her arm. And you will think your mom's burn looks like a map of rivers and lakes and places you'd like to go. And your mom will say, Stop it, and she will never wear short sleeves again. But you will always know the scar is there and will listen for your mom's lie when people in July say, Oh Marie, aren't you hot in that long-sleeved shirt? It must be ninety degrees out here. For heaven's sakes, put something cool on. No. No. I'm not hot, just prone to sunburn.

And you will learn to lie. She doesn't sing, she doesn't wear short sleeves. And there are other things.

But there are beautiful moments, too.

Sister Gertrude's flapping black habit heralded our march to the altar on First Holy Communion Day in second grade. Dad and Mom flanked me as my sixty-three classmates, their parents, and we processed into St. Mary's Church in Sleepy Eye.

Dad bent over me. "That old bat was probably at the Last Supper. She was teaching when I went to school here."

William, shhh, said Mom. But she smiled.

"Well, she was. She pulled our ears and twisted the girls'

hair. Do you remember that, Marie? She'd get it from me if she ever did that to you, Colie. The old battle ax. She'd get it all right."

I pressed my rosary-wrapped hands to my curling mouth and let the veil fall across my cheek to cover my sin. Giggling on First Holy Communion Day was blasphemous.

"Now don't drink too much wine. I don't want you getting goofy."

Dad, that's Jesus' blood, I whispered.

"Sure, Colie. That's right."

It soaked around the holes, then spread, staining Big Jenny's white fur first red and then dirty orange, like food coloring stretching in water. Deep in the middle, lighter on the periphery. He came down on her over and over in passionate eruption, in her neck, in her cheek and breaking through the bones, and in her neck again. She still stood in a striped coat of blood like a strange hybrid of pansies Mom planted once, dark and white and red. He stabbed at her flank and then near her ribs where the pitchfork sank in deepest as it found the cavity of her lungs and ripped through them. The pen opened up to a dank scent, like the odor released when a pile of rotting leaves is lifted and the dead grass wants for fresh air. She collapsed. Her head and front legs first. I backed up again against the calf to keep Big Jenny's head off my toes. She dripped blood and fluid from her nostrils and the holes and the holes and the holes. Dad kept at it. He aimed for organs. Her back finally lowered onto her bended hind legs.

When her entire weight was down, she tipped to the side and lay like a sleeping dog, legs reached out, chest huffing gently. I didn't look at Dad. I didn't want to fasten his eye or his mind or his memory to me. I ran from there silent to get Mom and left the calf to try reaching past the rope for its mother.

The evening was heavy with heat and seemed to drop several shades in the seconds it took to run from the barn to the house.

He's pitchforking her, I said. Mom picked up the baby from the high chair and left the potatoes boiling over and said, Oh shit, as she opened the screen door. She lugged Baby Natty on her hip and jogged to the barn. Annie Jo and I tagged behind.

What happened? What happened? Annie Jo asked. She pulled my sleeve.

Shhh, I said. Dad's killing Big Jenny.

Big Jenny gasped for breath though her lungs, collapsed by the prongs of the pitchfork, couldn't fill, and her calf, the knob-legged creature, called from the corner but nobody moved to answer him. We stood there and watched Dad pant with the exhaustion of stabbing the cow so many times, watched the cow suffocate in her own blood. Her ears shuddered flies off, and the black pests swarmed around the discharge of her eyes and nose. Mom handed Natty to me, told me to take my sisters back up to the house. I wound Natty around my hip and told Annie Jo to come on.

What have you done? Mom said to Dad. What in Christ's name have you done? I looked over my shoulder at them before we left the barn. Dad clasped his hands on the handle of the pitchfork and laid his forehead on them, and Mom raised her arms, lifted them as if to catch something falling from the loft, but nothing fell.

"Get out, goddamn you. Get out," Dad said. He pulled the pitchfork back over his shoulder, aimed at the swaying bulb, and darkened the pen with a blow.

Mom stopped coming to Dad's amateur games at Stark after my third sister was born in 1984. Mom told Dad that she thought the baby was coming today and that he should probably skip his game.

"I can't. It's Leavenworth and those bastards play smart ball. They need me. You'll be fine. Ma delivered us at home, for Christ's sakes."

Labor came on while Dad played in the game, and when the guy running the concession stand told me to run and tell Dad that it was Mom's time, I snuck into the fence that curled around the diamond, stepped down into the dugout, sat beside Dad, and whispered that the baby was coming. He told me to just wait and to get out. I did. After the game, the players gathered around Dad to listen to him tell stories of the Red Sox's famed catcher, Carleton Fisk, hitting that homerun in the bottom of the twelfth inning in the 1975 series and how he had been on standby, ready to jump in and take Fisk's place behind the plate that whole season if that knee of his roared with pain one more time and how Dad had played one game in the majors and caught for Luis Tiant. The stories became more detailed and elaborate as the years passed and the beers spilled and the faces changed, and sometimes I saw the players look at each other and smirk and then I took my sisters away from there to play hotbox or catch poppers on the empty field. After Dad's exhaustion of stories, we went home.

That day, Mom stood in the kitchen with the phone held to her ear with one hand and the other around her belly. Her feet stood wide apart and a pink pool of water spread at them. Colie, watch the girls until Grandma gets here. We've got to go. Dad, still in uniform, drove her to the hospital, and Lila, his fourth daughter, burst through Mom thirty minutes later.

Grandma went to all of Dad's games, but she never got out of her brown Chevy Impala to sit in the grandstands with the rest of the fans. She cross-stitched roosters on flour-sack dish towels and honked the horn whenever Dad trapped a dusty pitch in his glove, the same glove he used those years playing for the Sox. He only switched years later when Terry Steinbach—fellow southern Minnesotan, catcher for the Oakland Athletics, and friend of Dad's—sent him one of his. Then he used that. Terry Steinbach's name stitched in gold letters shone against the black leather.

> I am sitting with two of Stark's most famous sons, Darrell and Duane Helget. They have five other brothers and many more cousins—I'm given the names of seventeen Helgets in all—and they all love baseball. . . .

> *Oh, they were good. William Helget caught in the Red
> Sox organization for several years and Vic Helget was a
> fantastic pitcher. . . .*
>
> *And dedicated? Whew. The Helgets were dairy farm-
> ers, which is about the most demanding, unforgiving job
> there is. Those cows must be milked twice a day, every
> day, no matter what, and, by God, the Helgets milked
> them by hand!*
>
> JIM CAPLE, ESPN "Baseball the Way
> It Ought to Be," August 12, 2002

Dad didn't go to Stark the night of Jim Caple's visit. He said
he wasn't interested in it anymore. Years had passed in a suc-
cession of daughters, crops, and seasons, and when he real-
ized he was playing with kids half his age, he quit baseball.
Other players from other teams came to visit our farm,
stopped and asked him if he would coach them, and he said
no to all, said he was done with and tired of it. He said he was
going to focus on farming and watch a few of his daughters'
softball games.

Grandma said it was a regular tragedy that Mom couldn't get
at least one son for Dad and said they should've kept trying for
the Helget boy who would wear the name, the face, the legs,
the voice, and play the game. It's not the same in a girl, she
said when she looked at me. But my last sister, born in 1993,
almost killed Mom, and the doctors closed her womb forever.
Six daughters would be the legacy of a man with six brothers.

· · ·

When I reached the house with Baby Natty on my hip and Annie Jo tailing behind crying for poor Big Jenny, I set them up at the table. I turned off the potatoes, gray from cooking without water all that time, and pulled the roast from the oven. They ate. I called Grandma.

Grandma, I think you should come over and help Mom. Dad killed Big Jenny.

What do you mean, now?

He was trying to get her out of the pen but she wouldn't leave the calf, and Dad killed her with the pitchfork.

There was a long pause.

Now, listen here. You just mind your business and don't say a word about it. It's just a cow. You hear me? Those cows can drive any man to madness. Run down there, and tell your dad to let the blood out before she rots. Save the meat of her. Not a word about it, though. Tell your ma to call the butcher over in LaSalle. He's decent.

Okay, Grandma.

Okay, then.

Cruelty is close to curiosity. What happens when you zip kittens into a duffel bag and leave them bake on the deck in August? How does it feel to stretch the neck of a chicken and slice head from body while the orange legs claw at the air? How peculiar will it be when you pull the innards from that chicken, still warm, and the heart seems to beat even as the head, feet, and feathers are gone and scattered about the yard? If you throw a cat from the hay loft, will it land on its feet? What about from the top of the drying bin? Can a kitten get out of a bucket of oil as fast as it scrambles out of a sink full of water? If you crack a hen's egg, past eating stage but before hatching, what will be inside? How long will spray paint stay on the dog's coat? How far can you poke a stick up the nose of the stillborn calf? And will you dare touch the glassy eye with your bare finger? How many pellets does it take to kill a pigeon? Just once if you get it in the head, ten in the breast? If you clasp a pliers hard on the dog's ear, how long before he bites you and you run off to tell your dad and your dad swings at that dog with a baseball bat? How many pellets for a sparrow? And will your aim be good enough for them, the fast and flighty things that soil all over your dad's machinery? How much insecticide will it take to kill the grinding, burrowing, eating maggots erasing the decomposing favorite cat of your sister? And will you drag her behind the door in the feed room to see it and force her head close to this cat, her favorite, the one she named Mousey, by pushing your hand on the back of her neck until her long hair coils into one perfect curl on the belly of the dead thing pulsating with larval chaos? Will you tell your sister that the white worms will climb her hair and make a home on her head and in her ears? Will you make her pet the tail and hold her hand there until the maggots feel her palm? You will learn. So many things will be at your mercy.

I sat on an upside down, five-gallon insecticide pail while I waited for Dad to drive the loader tractor in. Dad drove slow over the gravel, and Big Jenny, dangling from a chain wound around her back legs from the loader's stretched bucket, dragged a dead resistance against the ground with her two front hooves. She left a bloody route from the barn to the machine shed, where we would bleed her completely. Dad killed the engine of the tractor and stepped down to the dirt floor. He patted the cow's back and poked her belly to see if she was toughening. Already her body firmed with the stopped blood in her veins and threatened rotting the muscle, the meat. Her udder, so full, still leaked milky diamonds. Dad walked behind me and fumbled around on his work bench until he found a hunting knife in a Folger's coffee can filled with scalpels, cutters, and blades for opening seed bags and slicing wires.

"Back up, now. She might splatter," he said to me.

He straddled the cow's head between his knees, held it in place steady with his legs, and opened up her neck with a slow separating of fur, skin, tendon, and muscle. He didn't rush. He cut her deep, but the ferocity was gone. The blood surged from her, and when the flow slowed, Dad told me to grab a hoof and hoist it as high as we could to get the blood to drain from the front legs, too. I got off the pail and stepped into the red-soaked gravel under her. Puddles of blood sat where the ground was too stubborn. Dad helped me get Big Jenny's leg up into the air, showed me to use my head to help hold the burden. We spread the cow's body. She would go to the meat locker in La Salle, a tiny town south of us, because the guy knew Dad and surely had seen this sort of thing before. Probably, the butcher wouldn't ask questions when he saw the holes gaping the cow's face, in her nostrils, in her neck, in her side, and flank, and breast, and in the organs that he wouldn't be able to salvage for anything other than grinding into sausage because they were so mutilated with puncture wounds. The butcher knew what it was to get a feel for the slicing and penetrating and tearing of flesh.

Dad washed the blood from my shoes and feet with the garden hose.

"Gets sticky, doesn't it, Colie? Get between your toes."

Dad left this place and this life when I was eighteen and the youngest, Mia, was one. He disappeared somewhere suffering with himself, I imagine. In those years, he missed first days of kindergarten, Holy Communions, high school graduations, college days, weddings, and the births of five grandchildren, four of them boys. After he left, Mom stoked a fire that sent all Dad's clothes, his baseball uniforms, and his bats with the name *William Helget* burned on the barrels of them twirling into the air on an ascending veil of black smoke. What's left is a wide open grassy place where six sisters and their children stretch and play baseball.

Plant your feet, Mitchell, I say to my six-year-old. You can't be twirling like a ballerina there if you want to hit it.

I know, Mom, he says.

Well then stop doing it.

Come *on*, Mitchell, says Isabella. I'm bored to death out here. She wears her mitt on her head, picks at the grass. She's seven, the oldest, and queen of all things pink. But she's the one who looks Indian, and Gypsy, and German. She's dark and lean and has a storm brewing beneath her beauty. Her face is mine, is Dad's, is Grandma's.

You just get in your stance and get ready, I say. Mind your business.

Mitchell takes a practice swing. He tries to hit a dancing butterfly with his bat.

Get your head in it now, Mitchell. It's 90 percent mental. Picture how it should look getting whacked out there to center field. Then put your body behind it.

I'm gonna pretend it's Phillip's big head, he says.

No, you're not. He's two and you do not have fantasies about swinging bats at your brother's head. Got it?

I fix Phillip behind me, the place he should stand so he doesn't get hit. I pitch and Mitchell swings and he misses and there is no one to catch the ball and to pull it in and to say, Nice one, Colie. It just rolls away over the earth, getting lost in the old pasture.

Blood saturates this place, your home. From butchering the chickens, and gutting the deer, and shooting the puppies, and stabbing the cow, and feeding the dogs the fly-breeding flesh of dead animals dropped by the rendering truck, and exploding a rabid raccoon, and breaking birth on the kitchen floor, and thawing bleeding steaks on the counter, and beginning the bloody months six times, and rinsing bloody panties that expose first experiences with boys, and the collecting blood that bruises the skin under eyes or on arms from hits or swings or baseballs, and saying Amen for the priest whose white robe drips with the blood of history when he challenges you eye to eye and presents the chalice and says, Blood of Christ. Water to wine to blood. And you will drink it and hold his eye until the blood runs down your throat and spreads its strands around the Indian and the Gypsy and the German helixes that your dad built in you and that you have left on this place. It's a holy thing. You could pick up the ground here, let it run through your fingers, and it would stain you red.

Burn to Black

Flames leapt and reached and pulled and lashed against a middle-of-summer sky already sweltering, throbbing hot blue and white. Fire blurred into the hazy afternoon and erased all lines between blaze and day, as if they were inseparable. The machine shed wall wrinkled in repulsion against the heat. Tree leaves puckered and bark blackened in response. I watched Mom stoke a fire so crotchety it seemed the devil, himself, had punched a hole through the ground and commenced pole-vaulting on his red forked tail. It was a fire to burn every memory of Dad into dead ash.

The fire started with just one small letter, a note from a woman that my sister found in Dad's pants pocket before laundry. *Chief,* it said, *I had a wonderful time with you. Thank you for dinner and all that came after. Especially, for being so good to me. I hope you are able to get away next weekend. I love you and miss you, Sandy.*

Like a great hand, the fire summoned wind into itself intense enough to suck us all, Dad's six daughters, into the fire waltz and force us to coil with the devil for all eternity if we weren't careful. Black clouds, weighted with soot, twisted from the fever, lifted above the grove, and beckoned neighbors to put down their farming chores and come and see what got into Mom this time.

When Mom went wild, neighbors crept up like curious cats, toms missing pieces of their ears or tails for their nosiness, to watch her antics. She broomed-down naughty dogs until they'd be still or die, mowed lawn nine months pregnant in a tube top and braless, pushed over dead trees with the loader tractor, pulled to life the chainsaw because she liked the smell, and screamed above the cottonwood trees and all things growing at Dad or the rest of us. Mostly, I think, it had always been entertaining for the neighbors, but sometimes their wives would send them over to pack my sisters and me into the beds of their trucks to get us out of the way for a while until Mom settled down with a rage and a cry and a bath and a nap. Then the neighbors fed us bread and ground cherry jelly and let us play with their calves, and we wondered if we could stay for a bit longer. As I got older, the neighbors said things to me like, You do a fine job managing all those little sisters, Colie. You sure are a help to your mother. And they stopped coming by as often.

But, bid by the black smoke, Lloydy Brown, Rabbit Hoffman, and Dukey Kral came the day Mom started the fire from the letter. They drove past our place at first, slow for a good look, before they pulled in our field road just past our driveway, backed out, and decided to crawl their pickup into our yard for certain. They had to be careful with Mom, they knew. Had to approach her gently. They piled out of the truck, one behind the other, led by Rabbit, and watched us file from the house to the fire carrying Dad's belongings for a good five minutes before saying anything.

Hey, Colie. What ya' doin'? Rabbit asked me.

Burning stuff, I said.

Well for Christ's sakes, Colie, I can see that myself. Marie. What in the name of God are you doin'? The smoke's about to black out the sun in case you haven't noticed it.

Mom said for him to go home.

Lloydy said to Rabbit and Dukey that he heard Chief left Marie and the girls for good this time. Got himself a woman, a bankteller over in Rochester. He said this loud enough for us to hear. He wanted to be corrected, I believed. But we didn't say anything, just kept lugging Dad's mementos to that fire, kept tossing them in. Yellow work gloves, his baseball cards, white Fruit of the Looms, long red-striped socks, plaid shirts, leather work boots, his feather pillow, a box of free caps he got from the seed dealer, Old Spice, his bowling shirt. We watched them blaze up and die.

Yep. That's what I heard too, said Dukey. He leaned to Rabbit, said, But Marie's a tough woman to live with. And six daughters? That'd drive the best of us running.

Lloydy thought he could talk Mom out of burning to black all Dad's stuff.

Chief's gonna want that bat, he said. You shouldn't be burnin' his baseball bat.

But she looked through him. She marched past and didn't entertain his nervous smile. She hurled the bat onto the burning heap with all the experience of a baton twirler. Mom had been head cheerleader in high school and could handle a baton like nobody's business, Dad once said. He sometimes said things like that about Mom when kindness was in him and Mom was tame. The bat twirled a few times before landing with a puff of black ash and spark.

The bat, Dad's from his years with the Red Sox as a catcher, was lean like a long wooden leg. On the barrel of it the name *William Helget* stared back at us before an ash coat settled on it and turned it unreadable.

I'm burnin' it all, she said. Especially that bat. He thinks he's too good for this, for me. Thought he could've been a pro and that I held him back. What a joke. It's all going. Every shittin' thing of his left on this place, that bastard. I don't want nothing of his. Nothing.

And Lloydy looked to me, and then panned the yard at my sisters, all the dark hair and skin of them, all the stages of them—baby to me, an adult practically—one, two, eight, eleven, fourteen, and eighteen years old.

I just don't want you to have any regrets, Marie, said Lloydy. You can't smoke the man out entirely. That's all. We're worried about you and the girls. I'll take 'em over to the wife for a while and get them out of your hair, okay?

Nobody's going anywhere, she said. Nowhere. You are not taking these girls.

Lloydy stepped back. Mom pushed a hair strand from her face, left a smudge of black on her brow.

They're not going anywhere, she said again.

We heaved boxes and bags full of clothes and bowling trophies onto that fire. We hauled shoes, pictures, books, blue jeans, coveralls, cleats, baseball gloves, and magazines and tossed them into the flames, too. When Rabbit said, I've had enough of this nonsense, and ran for the garden hose, Mom called out, Stop! with enough conviction to keep him from turning on the water even though Mom was just a bitty thing barely over five feet while Rabbit's hand alone was big enough to palm watermelons.

Dukey and Lloydy and Rabbit stayed for the hours it took us to clean the house of Dad's memory. They watched us lug his desk, full of farm and business papers, through the sliding glass door, drop it down the deck steps, and tug it across the yard to the fire. They didn't make a move to help, but they didn't interfere either. And they didn't chase the papers that flew about the yard and escaped on the wind.

At last, all that was left was Mom and us, dark and red with heat and soot and tan, the three neighbors hanging in the back, quiet now, and the fire. Mom breathed deep and looked alive then, standing before the flames as if she commanded the power of it with glare and will. Her curly hair danced and her eyes glowed. And, again, the devil tapped happy in the middle of the inferno.

Mom picked up the baby, Mia, the youngest of us, from the ground where she'd been sucking on rocks and held her at arm's length. Mia reached back to turn her face from the fire, to try cuddling into Mom's breast. But Mom held her firm toward the red and orange fervor.

Mom, I said.

The baby's body recoiled from the fire. Her legs and arms kicked and sprawled. She let out a howl, took in a mouthful of smoke and heat, choked, then coughed.

Watch, Mom said.

She turned to each of us, caught Dakota's alfalfa green eyes, Lila's clay ones, Natty's coon black, Annie Jo's dirty-straw amber, and my old leather color. Our eyes reflected in the building blue thunderheads of Mom's irises, cast eerie weather across her gaze. Under Mia's armpits, Mom's hands held fast. Mia's eyes, still milky gray with babyhood, but turning to Dad's dark earthly colors rather than Mom's light sky hue sure enough, faced the fire.

Watch this, she said again. She nodded to the flames.

Watch this and then forget.

Cockleburs in the Laundry

(SUMMER 1984)

A dresser drawer slams shut, drops a hollow echo down the stairs. A roar of thunder drums the window where Little Natty's been smearing drool, scares her to a cry. Mom sighs.

I need a pair of socks, Dad calls, and I'm almost out of underwear.

Well, Mom yells, do you think I don't know it? We have a little crisis, for crying out loud. Cockleburs in the laundry, in the whites.

Dad treads down in work jeans, flannel shirt. Hairy bare feet. Mom, dishtowel wrapped around her head for a scarf and squat on the floor, lifts a handful of loose socks, a bra, and a pair of Dad's briefs for evidence. The brown weed bunches sock cotton together, pokes out from the hem of a T-shirt, the elastic of panties, binds the wide band of Dad's Fruit of the Looms, fastens her camisole strap to his long underwear. A cocklebur stuck to a pant leg or dog's ears is a nuisance; a frenzy of cockleburs spun about in the wash and dryer is a menace, about as easy to collect as a colony of ants in the baking cupboard.

A wedding photo of Dad and Mom hides under old farm papers in the bottom drawer of the oak hutch (she tore all their wedding pictures down from walls, off dressers and coffee tables one Sunday morning in a temper, smashed the glass of the frames, said she was tossing the photos in the burn barrel—but she hid them here, a sweet secret she won't let Dad know she's kept. I see her, sometimes, bent over them, looking, when she's supposed to be hunting for receipts or titles or whatnot). The photographer posed Mom's hand, spread like steps, knuckle to knuckle, over Dad's, which looks awkward, like he's embarrassed to have so much attention paid to his hand, the bones edging up through the skin not for work but for posturing. Her hand's veinless, ceramic, white, and long red-nailed. I picture Mom's sister holding that palm in hers and waving a small brush over Mom's nails the night before this wedding and saying, Be still now so that I don't smear this all over. Pretty color, this red. Camaro, it's called. Dad's hand is already rough like a good man's ought to be, tan, and his nails have been bitten, it's obvious. Besides the red nail polish, the silver rings are new (the wedding bands sit in a Cool Whip container now, along with loose change, bolts, nuts, pins, and other junk emptied from pockets before laundry—neither wears their ring. Dad says his could get caught on something—an auger, PTO shaft, pull-rope—and rip his finger clean off. Mom says she got too full up with fluid when she got pregnant with Natty).

Dad sweeps his foot through the pile of laundry strewn about the floor. Well for Christ's sakes, Dad says. I've got to have a pair of socks. Here. Skootch over. Let me help.

Mom moves, sweeps clothes from floor space for Dad with her arm. Dad sits cross-legged. He's used to bending, crouching for milking and from baseball. Their knees touch.

Now, how'd you manage this damn mess? he says.

Oh, I don't know, but there are cockleburs fixed in everything. Must've stuck on the girls' socks while they were traipsing through the grove after that tom cat yesterday. I didn't think to check their clothes for cockleburs before I threw in the laundry. Who thinks to check for cockleburs?

Well, not you, I guess, he says.

Dad matches a pair of his socks, yanks one over his foot, then the other.

Ah, Christ, he says.

He takes that one off again, reaches deep inside to pull a wadded cocklebur seed from the toe.

I wouldn't've either, probably, Dad says.

You don't have to do this, Mom says.

Oh, it's wet out there anyway. Can't get much work done with the sloughs all over the fields and the rain still comin' through tomorrow, the weather man said.

Ignoring us girls, ignoring the cows, and the clouds dropping their weight, Dad and Mom pick the barbs, the dry hooks hiding in all the creases and hems, shake them off their fingers and onto a dryer sheet Mom's set aside. They pull the earthy needles from towels. Dad's fingers, as dainty as he can manage, pluck slivers from Natty's little socks, my panties, Annie Jo's pajamas; Mom's nails, not Camaro red anymore but still long, get the thorns that his thick fingers, nails bitten to the quick, can't seem to pinch.

Brewing

(SUMMER 1982)

Moonshine's Potato Mash Whiskey

Potatoes, skinned and diced

Boiling water

Yeast

Sugar

Corn Syrup

Malt

Mix all ingredients. Move the mash into a still and leave to ferment. You can smell when it's ready. Heat to vapor and until the liquid produced is clear. Then you know it's time to trap the condensation on the worm. That condensation hanging on it is the moonshine ready for drinking. Save the mash and reuse.

Moonshine's dogs, Wreck and Bump, shed globs of hair and drooled black ooze. Their jowls bore Rottweiler characteristics, along with their brown eyebrows and short and thick noses. The rest of them might have been some corruption of black lab, lean bodies with black coats interrupted here and there by bald spots and matted clumps. Mutts of this sort ran all over our townships of Albin and Stark, south of Sleepy Eye in southern Minnesota, because breeding was pretty much left unchecked by farmers, Catholics mostly, who felt wrong in denying anything, even dogs, their reproductive ways.

Moonshine farmed the eighty to the east of us. He had bought that eighty, some of the richest soil north of the Little Cottonwood River, off Henry Fischer but only after Moonshine agreed to marry his oldest daughter, Clara, a solid-hipped German girl whose cooking apologized for the temper she inherited from her dad. Moonshine set aside three of those acres for growing potatoes and made the corn, soybean, and alfalfa growers wonder about his sanity, especially since half the potato field was dug up in a fury and eaten raw by Wreck and Bump.

Mom said not to touch those mangy mutts, they're full of disease and spite. They traveled together from farm to farm trying to mate cats, chase kids, and swipe chickens. They drank oil, too.

They can't taste a thing, Dad said, because Moonshine feeds those dogs his homemade brew. A little engine oil isn't nothing to them because they've got goat stomachs.

Wreck and Bump headed for our pails of drained oil first thing when they came moseying into our yard, a spectacle of bastard features, caulker burs, and goiters on legs crossing scissors-like. Mom said it was a wonder they could move at all they were so crooked. Shameless. Feeding that whiskey to poor dumb animals who don't know any better.

Mom told me to phone and tell Clara to send Moonshine over to pick up his dogs because they were in our chickens again. Clara said he'd be right over and did we need any ground cherry jelly? Mom bundled two loaves of banana bread in a dish towel. From our kitchen window, open to the Little Cottonwood River wind, I watched Wreck and Bump scattering chickens and feathers out of the coop. Moving hot oil–like between chickens, the pair of them sent the white girls popping and clucking. Our own mutts, Otis and Pierps, sulked in the shadow of the milking barn hoping not to be pestered. Ours were a worthless pair with not much more sense than Wreck and Bump and even less ambition, but Dad always scratched their bellies, poured beer into their water, and picked ticks and cottonwood seeds out of their ears. When the cottonwood trees went to seed, the whole county went thick white.

Moonshine drove in on his John Deere 4010 that leaked fluids galore from the hydraulics. He liked to travel that way. Thought it saved him gas. Wreck poked his nose out from the coop, feathers stuck to the gummed oil around his mouth, and Bump stopped his mischief and sat on the coop ramp chomping a sorry chicken between his jaws. Red stained the white feathers, though the beak still moved to silent clucks and its orange legs cycled on.

Mom, I said, there goes another one.

She looked over my shoulder and out the window.

Oh shit, she said. Well, feed it to the cats, I suppose. Get out there now and give these loaves to Moonshine. Tell them they're for Clara and not to be eaten until he gets home and don't linger or he'll be here all the livelong day and you've got laundry to fold.

I took them from Mom, opened the screen door, and heard Moonshine yell to his dogs. *Wreck. Bump. Get over here you little bastards and I don't mean maybe.* He rose from his seat and called them again over the noise and hood. *Why you leave those chickens be. Put that down now, damn you.*

Moonshine's face furrowed like field rows around his eyes and sprouted rogue hairs from his nose, and I put him to be about eighty the whole time I knew him, eighteen years or so. The only thing that ever changed was the color of his nose, which was usually browned, not with tan, but with soot and dirt and hair. It would redden to tomato in high summer. He killed the tractor engine and waved as I walked across the yard. He wore the type of overalls only farm stores carry, stiff denim ones with white stripes running up and down, but Moonshine's were at least five sizes smaller than anyone else's, corn stalk thin as he was. Talk had it that a Chicago jail housed Moonshine for bootlegging before he settled here and married Clara, and I always imagined he escaped and wore those prison-looking clothes as a sort of penance for his crime and might've married Clara for the same reason, penance.

Chicago's speakeasy booze came right out of these fields,

Dad said to me, and out of Minnesota stills hidden under pig sties and calf pens. Ah Colie, you'd be surprised at how these old farmers really made their money. Running whiskey for some Chicago gangster is how Moonshine came to know the place, this place, and why he came back to it after prison.

Moonshine kept a handkerchief in his pocket, white and lacy like a woman would use. Dad figured he used that kind because he was Irish and the Irish were odd as hell and mostly too drunk and too mindful of Pope John Paul the Second to think clear like the rest of us. I hoped maybe some fair-skinned, dark-haired, blue-eyed woman named Shannon or Erin or Kathleen dabbed it with vanilla and slipped it to him on a prison visit and that they became separated or she died giving birth to his baby or she went back to Ireland, say, to marry another or something beautifully tragic and Moonshine carried her lace handkerchief for memory and all Clara's yelling didn't matter to him because he had this woman once, even if all he had now was her handkerchief to carry in his pocket and smell once in a while. Vanilla's a lingering scent.

Wreck and Bump bounded for me and I held the bread up high, as I was only seven and short besides. Bump dropped the chicken at my feet, maybe for an exchange of bounty. The two circled around my legs and nipped at my knees. I kept walking through their antics. I had learned that if I stopped moving, Wreck and Bump would take it as an invitation to hump my legs or jump up and slap front paws on my shoulders.

Hey there, Colie-girl. I see you found my dogs. Haven't been any trouble, have they?

No, Moonshine, I said. They've been good as gold, but Mom doesn't like them getting into her chickens. She said for you to give these loaves to Clara.

Why, thank you. These'll be mighty fine, I'm sure. Your ma bakes real nice. She got any of those caramel rolls with the pecans in there?

He tilted his head toward the house, peeled back a corner of the dish towel, and took a whiff of the bread. He replaced the corner, set the bundle at his dirty boots, next to two jars of yellow jelly and a mason jar of clear liquid still sloshing from the ride over.

Lightning's Corn Whiskey

Corn meal
Barley
Rye
Sugar
Boiling water
Yeast

Pour the boiling water over the yeast. Mix in the corn meal, barley, rye, and sugar. Leave to ferment a few days, then heat to bubbling. The liquid on top should be the color of beer. Then trap the vapor in a tube or run it on a coil. Keep the slop and just add more sugar, water, grains, and corn for the next batch. This batch will be stronger because of the old mash.

Moonshine's not the only guy cooking mash. Everybody's brewing something out here. To the west, we've got Lightning and Flossie Sellner. Once after we helped them gather their roaming steers, the ancient pair tugged up crocks full of homemade corn whiskey from their basement. When Flossie's herd got out, the whole section joined in the round-up. Lightning and Flossie raised sixty steers for slaughter, and those steers had their run of the Little Cottonwood River bank. Lightning rigged up an electrical fence around the pasture and counted on the river as boundary for the west line. In '88, rain clouds didn't shape, the sun smoked the water and exposed flopping bullheads to the curious eyes of Flossie's steers. It's a fact that cows will try to eat anything once, and I don't know if it was the appetizing way the moon glinted off slick fish bodies or intense hunger or just plain nosiness that enticed those steers into that dry river bed, but all sixty of them slid down the bank, sniffed and tasted fish, and climbed up and out the other side before morning. Chewed bullhead bits lay everywhere. Free and sated from the fish feed, the steers wandered into corn and soybean fields, over gravel roads, onto homesteads, and into open machine sheds. When morning woke, men gathered in groups, removed caps and pointed this way and that with them, while the women buzzed on the phones about who was going to bring what over to Sellners. Any neighbor who could spare time, equipment, and labor set aside work, packed up wives, sons, dogs, and daughters into pickups, and headed to Sellners, even though Lightning and Flossie stayed to themselves and weren't the neighborly sort. They never attended baseball games or church and didn't swap garden goods. And Flossie used to point at my sisters and me with a .22 when we pedaled past her place on our way to the Little Cottonwood River Bridge, the bridge where we hung our fishing lines for carp and bullheads and spray-painted initials and poems and swear words on the concrete supports. Sometimes Flossie fired a warning shot into the air that knocked her back a step, got us pumping our legs like the devil himself was licking our heels, and sent the steers into fits of calling and bucking.

She don't mean nothing by it, Dad always said, she's just mad the county split her farm in half with that new tar road. What would she wanna shoot a scrawny pack of Indians like you for?

Dad shooed Mom, my sisters Annie Jo and Natty, and me outside and said to get going. We knew how to bring in cows and weren't afraid of steers. Castration removed the angst from them a long time ago. Mom and Natty clapped their hands at a steer chomping cabbage in our garden, and Annie Jo and I helped Dad lure two out of the corn granary. We walked those three steers back to Lightning and Flossie's place, and neighbors from all around were driving in the same. It was a convergence of women, men, children, and sixty steers, every last one of them, there in Sellner's pasture. And when the men saw Lightning, heavy with years of beef and potato suppers and bent with labored age, digging holes and pounding poles for new fencing along the river boundary, they patted him on the back and took the dowel digger and sledge hammer from his hands. Lightning's eyes, lashless and half covered by sagging skin, met theirs, and he nodded. He picked his way across the pasture, up to the house where the women had already spread out breads, cheese, summerwurst, and jelly, went to his basement, and hauled up his best brew. He positioned the bottles on a board the women had laid across two empty gas barrels. The men drew in after the fence crept the entire spread of the west line.

Wreck and Bump barked with recognition when Moonshine leaned over and picked up his mason jar, whipped the handkerchief out from his pocket, and wiped the jar clean.

Be still now, Moonshine said to his dogs. You've been devils today and now I suppose you think you're going to get a bit of this. You'd better guess again. Now what about those rolls? he asked me.

Wreck lay at my feet and Bump settled in the shade of the tractor's middle.

No, she don't have any caramel rolls left, I said. We ate them all and Mom said she won't make anymore because Annie Jo and me have too many cavities.

Let me see, there. Open up.

I opened my mouth wide and let Moonshine take a look.

Well, I'll be, he said. He stepped down to the ground, kicked Bump out of his way. Have a look at this. He opened his mouth, leaned over me. Inside were seven or eight teeth the color and size of coffee beans. I get along just fine with these. Just have to do more drinking than eating is all.

I knew he wasn't kidding. Moonshine's still under his barn was no secret. Many nights the easterly breeze sent Clara's hollering for Moonshine to get out of that still right through our living room window. When she was really mad, she started yelling in German words I'd only heard my dad yell at a bad umpire or stubborn cow.

Between Moonshine's liking for whiskey and Clara's stubbornness there is plenty of room for troubles, Mom said. That whiskey's a terrible thing.

She said this low and into her chest usually, but I knew she was really talking to Dad, and in an indirect sort of way she was talking about him. Dad had been in the doghouse since he didn't come home from his baseball game on time the week before. Mom sat up all night waiting, and when he still wasn't home by the milking time the next morning, she fixed his breakfast, put it in the porch, and locked the doors of the house. Dad slept it off out there, and when the bellowing of the cows finally woke him, he ate his breakfast cold and headed to the barn, still in his baseball uniform. She didn't let him in again until supper time and didn't speak to him directly for three days. She said things to me like, *Tell your dad supper's on the table, The TV's too loud,* or *Grandma's on the phone. Did you call the meat locker? Can we get a side of beef? Fried or boiled potatoes for supper tonight?* I wondered if Clara asked Moonshine these ordinary sorts of questions in between ordering him to get from one place to another.

Clara never seemed to know exactly where she wanted Moonshine to go when her temper was hot, though. Her voice just followed him from wherever he was to somewhere else she didn't want him to be. Moonshine would start belting some silly but lonely-sounding song, the kind, Dad said, all the Irish sing when they're drunk or sad, above Clara's yelling, and sometimes he fired up that 4010 and took a drive around the section, past our place, past the Braulicks', by the rock fence of Annie Mary Twente's grave, on up to the Fischers', over the bridge and past the Little Red Schoolhouse where Clara used to teach the primary grades. Wreck and Bump either zigzagged after or rode in the rock box of the tractor. Together, they heralded Moonshine's escape, their tongues and ears flapping like victory flags in the winds of the Minnesota afternoons.

Driving over to our place on Clara's errands or at Mom's beckoning was a holiday for Moonshine, too. Mom had stopped going out to swap jars with Moonshine a long time ago and only called for him to pick up his dogs if Wreck and Bump got into the chickens because she could never get rid of him. He would stay all day talking about potato leaf hoppers, the Pope's bad health, Father Richter's sermon, the cost of corn syrup. She said she didn't want to encourage his nonsense. That's why she sent me out to get the jam and give him the loaves. He put the loaves on the fender of the tractor and unscrewed the lid of the shine jar. Wreck and Bump about danced on their tails, but they kept their rumps to the ground. They had to be good to get a bit, they knew. It was clear as liquid glass, clearer than our rusty well-water for sure. He handed the lid to me and told me, Have a lick. I brought the lid to my nose and gave it a smell. It bit my nostril but funneled down into my throat with a sweet sort of coating like the scent of burnt sugar. I touched my tongue lightly to the lid, drew it back into my mouth quick, and smiled when I looked at his old face.

Moonshine laughed, said, Ha! That's the syrup. Corn syrup. Just a bit of it for smoothness. Have just a sip now, a little nip. He handed the jar to me and gripped the metal buckles of his overalls.

He used Clara's jelly and pickle jars to hold his potato moonshine. I had probably clutched that very jar before when it housed some other preserved food swapped between Clara and Mom. Ground cherry jelly. Sweet corn relish. Strawberry jam. Dill pickles. Watermelon rinds. Red beets. This time, though, the jar felt lighter, daintier than my hay baling hands were used to. When it swirled, the clear liquid reflected the colors of everything I'd ever seen in my seven years. Stained glass in a jar.

Grandma Helget's Dandelion Wine
Dandelion blossoms
Boiling water
Cloves
Ginger
Orange juice and peel
Lemon juice and peel

Brewing

Lime juice

Sugar

Yeast

Pour boiling water over yeast. Mix rest of ingredients and bring to boil. Keep a running boil for a good hour. Strain through cheese cloth or coffee filter. Stir the yeast mixture into that drainage. Let stand overnight and pour into bottles or jars. Allow to breathe for a month. Then seal and store in basement or canning room.

Grandma Helget's a terrible woman, Mom said, but she can make a meal out of anything and wastes nothing and that's why your Grandma and Grandpa are rich and can afford to give a whole farm to your dad and each of your uncles.

Grandma Helget never liked Mom, a Haala. The Helgets had a feud going with the Haalas over a wintertime Sheephead card game back in the '40s when one of the Haala boys walloped one of the Helget boys over the head with a Christmas tree and stomped and strew wrapped presents about the floor. Ever since then, they've fought over land boundaries, baseball, homilies, and everything else, and a Romeo and Juliet marriage wasn't cute or romantic to anybody but Dad and Mom. Grandma said Mom was lazy, stupid, and fat. And she never could get a boy to come out of her. Not even one.

All those girls, six of 'em, Grandma said of us. They'd better make themselves useful.

For the first alfalfa cutting of the year, Grandma's seven boys gathered at the southernmost farm and worked their way north to the next six farms to cut, bale, and stack hay bales. Every brother helped the other.

That's the way we were raised, to work, goddamn it, Dad always said, we know how to work and we know where our loyalties are.

And each of those brothers towed behind him at least two or three sons, bare-chested boys scrawny as birds but useful all the same, to help with labor. When I turned nine, I could run the tractor and baler, but my uncles and boy cousins twitched with discomfort around me. Uncle Henry said it wasn't proper. Uncle Tweet said I was too young. Uncle Tubby said not to swear in front of me. Uncle Stretch said I was too rough with the clutch. Uncle Sue said I was too damn skinny and short for that tractor. Uncle Suck said to Dad, Chief, that girl belongs in the kitchen, fixing dinner with Ma.

And Dad agreed. After that, I helped Grandma prepare dinner for all those men and boys wet with summer and labor and speckled with bits of alfalfa leaves and dead bugs that drowned in the drops of sweat on their bodies. Grandma and I fixed ham and scalloped potatoes, goulash, beef roast and red potatoes, chicken noodle hot dish, and ring sausage and sauerkraut and set the boys up all over the porch at her house. I laid down towels and blankets for lounging and delivered pre-portioned plates. When Dad, Grandpa, my uncles, and boy cousins each had their plate, Grandma pulled the dandelion wine out from behind the stairs in the basement where she kept her canned goods and told me to get the glasses out of the hutch. Each of Grandma's seven boys and Grandpa wrapped a hand around a wine glass, crystal ones from the old country, filled with Grandma's homemade dandelion wine. My cousins got theirs in jelly jars, and Grandma mixed it with lemonade, so they didn't, as she said, lose their heads. After the men and boys ate, drank, and paraded out the drive for the next place, Grandma and I cleaned up and knocked back any leftover wine from the bottoms of those crystal glasses and jelly jars. Grandma wasn't so terrible then, I didn't think.

The aroma from Moonshine's mason jar alone could've sent me swirling, but I took a quick glance to the house to look for Mom and didn't see her, so I closed my eyes, put that jar up to my lips and drew in a taste. I swallowed in one fluid motion before I could change my mind. Moonshine grabbed the glass when he saw the liquor move down my neck, to make sure I didn't drop it, I suppose. I opened my eyes, and fire lighted there. Sparks of it singed my lips and the back of my throat on the thin skin. Where the membranes were thicker, the liquor smoothed over without burning, left a downy film of sugar and a flavor of something I liked but couldn't name. Vanilla or apple crisp or oven coils or Nut Goody candy bars or welded metal or molasses, maybe. I didn't know.

What did you think of that, little girl? Not bad, eh? He took a swig himself, wiped his mouth with his sleeve, and then set the jar on the ground. Wreck and Bump took turns lapping from it. First Wreck, then Bump, civil as churchgoers.

Moonshine opened the jar of ground cherry jelly, pulled his pliers from his pocket, and scooped a dollop onto it. He stuck it in my face.

Here, he said, have a little taste of this before you go back into the house to your ma. You don't want to get old Moonshine in trouble now, do you?

His lips curled around his gums in a smile. I licked it off.

When these jellies are all gone, you give a call over to Clara, and I'll bring you some more. Tell your mom thanks for the bread and sorry about the chickens.

He screwed the lid on the jelly jar and handed the both of them to me.

Moonshine picked up his mostly empty jar from the ground and tipped the last of it into his mouth. He put it in the rock box at the front of his tractor, then picked up Wreck and Bump and put them in, too. They sat easy and relaxed, smiling if dogs can smile. Moonshine climbed back into that 4010 and fired up a cloud of black diesel smoke.

Gerty Haala's Rhubarb Wine
Rhubarb, washed and chopped
Boiling water
Sugar
Raisins
Lemon

Pour boiling water over rhubarb. Let it soak for three days. Strain fruit through a cheese cloth. Add sugar and lemon and raisins to the juice. Cover and let stand for

nine days. Strain once more. Let stand for two months.
Then bottle and store in cool, dark place.

Minnesota soybean fields keep secrets. When Chester Haala, Mom's uncle and our other western neighbor, drank the day away cultivating his back forty, the soybean field didn't tell. When his four-year-old daughter wandered down the field drive, barefoot and bouncing, and lifted her arms to him for a ride and he plopped her up on the fender, the bean field didn't warn against it. When in his drunken haze, he took the end rows too fast and she slipped off the fender and sank under the wheel, the bean field didn't point and say, *he's drunk as hell and now he's killed that child.* It simply wrapped that secret in tangling bean vines, spread its velvety leaves over the stain in the earth, and never released a sound to us or to the passing cottonwood seeds flying overhead.

We kept secrets, too. Or, we pretended we didn't know things. In the Haalas' living room, the men poured rhubarb wine into Styrofoam cups meant for coffee, struck up Buck and Sheephead games, and shook their heads at the injustice of the terrible tractor accident and said, *Well at least it wasn't the boy,* and whispered, *Why wasn't Gerty keeping an eye on her? A woman's got to keep those little ones away from the machines.* And, *A man's got to get his work done, doesn't he? He can't be bothered with babysitting in the middle of field work, don't you know.* The women fluttered about the kitchen, made ham sandwiches and Special K bars, and encouraged everyone to eat, to keep their strength up. They told Gerty that there was plenty of time for another child. Just eat and have a sip of this they said to her. Gerty sagged and rocked on a chair near the fridge where her little girl's artwork, drawings of Big Bird and Ernie and attempts at her name, Carol, in bright crayon and backwards, hung secured by colored alphabet magnets. Gerty held Carol's blanket, a ratty pink thing with satiny edging, edging that Carol had rubbed under her eye until she fell asleep. *She called it her eye-eye, you know,* Gerty said. *This blanket, she called it her eye-eye. Why didn't I think to put it in the coffin? She'd have liked that. Oh why didn't I remember? What mother doesn't remember a thing like that? Her blanket. Why didn't I remember?* And then the sobs unsettled her, and she took to rocking again. C'mon now, Gerty. Have a drink of this to make you feel better. Take your mind off of it, they said. Nothing to be done about it. All you can do is just hold on to the ones you've got. There's no accounting for God taking the little ones. You just rest now, Gert. We'll take care of Chester and the boy for a few days until you're up to it again. Oh, but do you have this recipe handy, Gerty? You know, my ma used to make a rhubarb wine, too. Do you use brown sugar? Do you throw a couple of ground cherries in the mush? Ma used to, I think. It's good. It's real good. I'll pass another bottle around the living room for the men, the poor dears. They can't handle these things like a woman can. And all the women looked at each other, and they looked at Gerty holding that blanket, and every one of them found something to do—pouring, slicing, buttering, spreading, sweeping, washing, or drying—and they bit down on their lips to keep the red tears from giving them away. They made more sandwiches and bars and poured more rhubarb wine. Could someone run down and grab another jar? She keeps them in the canning room, I think. Isn't that right, Gerty? Pick the oldest batch. She's got the jars labeled.

I walked back to the house, ground cherry jelly jars in hand, and climbed the stairs to the porch, put a jar under my arm, reached for the door of the kitchen, and wondered if it would be locked, but it turned easy. I went in, saw Mom removing more loaves from the oven. I set the jars on the counter, unscrewed the one already opened by Moonshine and used my finger to ladle jelly on a slice of hot banana bread. I stood at the kitchen window and ate though my numb mouth didn't seem to taste things quite right. I cut another three slices from the loaf.

Don't ruin your appetite, young lady, Mom said, and that jelly is too sugary for you to be eating it up all the livelong day.

Okay, then, I said. But I still spread the jelly over the bread pieces. I watched out the window at Moonshine steering that green tractor out our driveway and onto the road. The Little Cottonwood River wind whipped up just then, tossed hair across my eyes, and sent a swarm of cottonwood seeds to flight. The white billows passed the kitchen window and clouded the screen. Their tendrils gripped air molecules and rode the random will of invisible waves daring them to hang on. When the seeds settled, Moonshine's tractor was gone.

I'd have wondered whether he had really been there at all or if it had just been some escape of my imagination but for the sound of Moonshine's handkerchief tickling my ear and the scent of lingering vanilla romancing my nose and the taste of corn syrup massaging my tongue and the smooth of a mason jar cooling my hands. And a sense of imminent things: of steers eating bullheads and crystal glasses bulging dandelions and soybeans shushing cottonwood seeds. There was much to come.

Brimstone

(SUMMER 1985)

On Sunday at St. Mary's Church in Sleepy Eye, Father John says to vote Republican. Dad, up one eyebrow and cross-armed, looks over my head, over Annie Jo's head, over Natty's head, and down the pew to Mom. She tries to shame Dad's glance, gives him her crinkled forehead that means he's supposed to behave, but Mom buries her mouth into Baby Lila's curls and grins. Mom doesn't look up again until she's stretched her mouth straight. Father John says we are either mortal sinners or crazy if we vote left. And he doesn't care how many generations of Democrats we Midwestern farmers have voted for, it's about time we got our noses out of our bank books and into our Bibles. The Catholic constituency needs to get behind the Republicans once and for all—unless our last name's Kennedy and then we can go ahead and do what we want and don't let a little old priest from a tiny parish going belly up because of parishioners who seem to have forgotten that tithing to the Church is a tax break stop us from being a Democrat as oblivious to the tenets of the Roman Catholic Church as a jungle Pigmy is mindless to his fiery doom for worshipping tree monkeys and poisonous frogs, Father John says. He smoothes his hair, black as Angus and slick with Vaseline or a can of holy chrism.

Then Father John booms a homily about babies getting their brains sucked out and arms ripped off during abortions. He lugs a slide projector into the aisle while three altar boys fly to unroll a white screen that fights against the pulling to snap tight again. A fury of boys in white robes toils up there and the whole flock of parishioners strains necks to see what commotion Father John has orchestrated for *this* Sunday and whisper and wonder whether this homily will be as fine a sermon as *last* Sunday when he got sidetracked from preaching about vocations for the priesthood and sisterhood and started in on the sins of masturbation and fornication and said out loud the word that brought blood to the faces of the Sunday Youth Group Choir and tightened the gray lips of the Council of Catholic Women and stirred nervous coughs from the Knights of Columbus — penis. He started sweating so he had to swab his forehead with his Lenten stole, purple, which spread a dark smudge, to which Dad murmured over my head, Annie Jo's head, and Natty's head to Mom, I bet that's not the first time that stole's had a wet spot, which caused Mom to snort before composing herself. Then she gave Dad a brow-down look. Knock it off.

Father John shoos the altar boys away, flaps his arms at the song leader, which means to dim the lights and start the music, pulls a clicker from under his robe, and aims at the projector, which shoots pictures of see-through babies, hardly a few days old in their mother's stomachs, onto the screen. He tap, tap, taps at the heart on the screen with a cane he's borrowed from front-pew Bernie Fischer, foot gone to the auger a couple harvests ago. Father John clicks to dead babies, their brains vacuumed out and skulls thin, but otherwise whole pretty much. Fingers, toes, eyelashes, thumb sucking, and such. And he points out the live Catholic babies in our church—Fatty Pants Braulick crawling over the pew, Mandy Spaeth crying for her pacifier, that bald little Heiderscheidt boy dog-drooling on a song book, Brittany Berkner getting her nose wiped, the Fischer baby chewing on a strand of his sister's hair, Anthony Schroepfer the Third gumming Cheerios, and Susie Raucsh spitting up Similac in the pew behind us, spreading an awful odor, and Father John says, Imagine it. Just imagine, people. The mothers of the babies squeeze or kiss them and Mom straightens Lila's dress like someone's about to take her picture and old women start to cry because they are imagining like Father John told them to. I squeeze my eyes for tears, too, so Father John doesn't think I'm heartless or a Democrat. I try to imagine all those big, fat, healthy babies brainless or armless or lost in the limbo with the black babies of Africa who've never even heard of Jesus and who haven't been baptized and who have to wait until the end of the world for Jesus to show them His mercy and let them into heaven if they've received enough prayers from the good

Catholics on earth. Father John says how nurses sometimes see aborted babies breathing in wastebaskets or moving their little fingers on the way to the incinerator, but they can't do anything about it to save them because the liberals are so protective of their precious women's rights and the nurse'll be sued or attacked by mobs of feminists and hippies and Democrats. It's a child, not a choice, he says. What about the child's rights? is what Father John wants to know. And I want to know then, too. What about the child's rights?

Jee-sus H. Christ, Dad says when we get in the car. That man is goddamned lunatic. How's a person supposed to eat after something like that? I don't go to church for brimstone or to be told how to vote. There are other issues, for Christ's sakes.

I worry then that Dad might be a Democrat bound for Hell, but I expect that Mom'll give him a look that'll change his mind and save his soul. But she just says, That reminds me. I'm out of Lila's formula. And I need eggs and butter besides.

Annie Jo says she wants some Hostess Twinkies and Natty says she'll take a box of animal crackers.

And how much is that gonna cost? These kids'll eat us out of house and home yet. A man can't hardly afford his own family anymore.

All I can think about are those picture slides of babies and the murderous Democrats responsible for their deaths. And I set my mind to stop abortion forever and save the souls of Mom and Dad and the Democrats besides when I'm old enough.

Courting the Milkman

(SUMMER 1988)

The milkman's truck barreled down our quarter-mile driveway, spread dust waves up either side of the ditch. Great
swells built over our white house, curled around the front
porch, where Mom had set the tomatoes to sun for supper
and where Annie Jo, Natty, and Lila were wrestling kittens
into bonnets made of orange tiger lilies popped from the garden when Mom wasn't looking. Bulging west across the yard,
dirt rolled over her in the strawberry patch and shaded the
granary so that Dad and I had to cover our eyes and close our
mouth, stop our nose from breathing. When it passed, we
leaned on our shovels and watched the truck stop fast in
front of the barn's milkroom, skid marks into the gravel like
four shiny ribbons. Otis and Pierps—our old mutts—and
Snuffy—our new one—got out of the shadow of the barn to
bark and pee on the tires. Snuffy had snapped life back into
the old pair since Dad's brother Henry came over when he

knew Mom was off to town getting groceries and not around to tell him that there was no way under heaven that those four puppies bouncing in the truck bed were staying, but, because Mom was gone, Uncle Henry opened his tail gate and shooed Snuffy and three puppy brothers off it and onto our grass before he jumped back into the driver's seat and peeled off for the road with all four barking after the smoky muffler and little Natty chasing after them to come back. Snuffy liked Natty combing his fur with Dad's hair brush and liked biting the tails of Otis and Pierps, and he decided he would stay on our farm even after his three brothers ran away to places Natty couldn't find them though she searched day and night a good week with a stick of summerwurst for bait and bale twine for stringing them together and bringing even Mom to feel sorry for her and say, Natty, you'd better learn not to get so attached to things or you'll have a life of misery.

When the dust passed through the pasture, the cows came to the fence to get a look and bob their heads and moo hello to the milkman, too. The truck door opened on the driver's side, away from Dad and me, and a thick leg wearing a tennis shoe stepped down to the running board. The dogs went wild on him, warned him not to get down from there.

Looks like we got us a new milkman, Colie, Dad said.

Here comes Mom, I said.

Mom, aimed at the granary, pushed her way across the yard with an ice cream pail of strawberries bobbing against her hip.

William, Mom said. You tell him to not drive in here like

that. Like a shittin' bat out of Hell. You better tell him, she said before she spun around and marched back into her garden. She started picking again, then stopped, stood, hollered over to us. Shut those dogs up, too.

Colie, why don't you go call those goddamn dogs off him so he can get his business done and doesn't think we're runnin' a wild Indian camp here.

Okay, Dad.

And tell him to slow down when he drives in here, for Christ's sakes.

I put down my shovel and ran over.

Snuffy, I yelled. Come here you goddamn Indian. Get down now.

Still all I could see was the milkman's shoe on the running board and the shadow of somebody who didn't look like our old milkman, Art, who drove slow in the driveway because he knew we had little girls and little dogs and little kittens here. Art knew, too, that Mom wouldn't want driveway dust getting all over her tomatoes sunning on the porch, her strawberry patch spreading wide and blooming berries the size of thumbs, her laundry drying crisp on the clothesline, or her girls' long hair, which she made sure she worked clean of knots every night before they went to bed. Art knew, too, that Mom would not be quiet about dust getting on her things and would likely raise a holy row with him if it did.

I rounded the front of the milk truck and saw the whole of the new milkman sitting in the driver's seat young and pale and stocky like a heavy soybean plant and not at all like the way my boy cousins and uncles and Dad looked. A row of fall corn stalks they were, long and lean bodies and dark skin and jagged knees and elbows.

What do you got so many dogs for? the new milkman asked. This a dog pound or what? He was smiling big and tapping his tennis shoes at the air that separated our dogs from his legs. Not to hurt them I could tell.

If you settle down the little one, they'll all sit still, I said.

I kicked Snuffy quiet, then picked him up, pulled his ear and told him, Be still for Christ's sakes. He moaned a bit, and when I put him to the ground, he looked back to Otis and Pierps and yipped something that made the two follow him back to the shadow of the barn where they'd all been hanging out their tongues in the first place until Snuffy got them excited about the milkman.

The new milkman hopped down, glanced at me sideways with eyes pale green as the velvet leafs plaguing Dad's fields.

Thanks a lot, he said. You've got quite a way with animals, I see. You must draw them in like Francis of Assisi with that gentleness. Pure magic.

I didn't say anything. I talked back to insults better than cleverness.

I'm Swing, he said.

Where's Art? I asked.

I followed Swing to the side of the truck where he unrolled the milk hose he'd hung up there loose and uneven after his last stop, not tight and level like Art'd always done.

Art's in Hawaii or Mexico or something. I don't know. I said my name's Swing. You're supposed to introduce yourself after I tell you my name. That's how it goes in civilized conversation.

Colie.

Colie. What kind of a name is that? Is it short for something? Sounds like a dog's name.

He crossed his arms and tucked his hands in his armpits.

Tell me you've got a whole name and not a dog's name, he said. What is it? Colette? Colleen?

It's short for Nicole. My sisters call me Colie because it's easier.

Well what's easy got to do with anything? It'd be easier for them to wet their diapers until they're thirty-five, but I bet you don't let them do that, do you?

No, I said. I took a step toward him and planted hands on hips. We train them when they're two already.

Well there you have it then, Nicole. Nicole. That's much better. That's nice. Very pretty. Why is a girl with such a pretty name so rough with her dogs?

He waited for me to answer, lifted his eyebrows, but I didn't say anything.

Seems like she should be gentle with them, he continued, and not be kicking and hitting little puppies. And young ladies shouldn't swear either.

He raised his brow again, then grinned a little on one corner of his mouth.

My own mother never uttered a bad word. Not one. Not

even when I put glue in the Thanksgiving mashed potatoes. She just said, Eddie, that will be enough of you for this holiday. Up to your room now. And she whipped out a box of instant potatoes and saved the day without breaking a sweat or *Jesus Christing* this or *Goddamning* that.

He waited with his eyebrows raised again, and he waited so long that I had to say something or run away from there ashamed.

Hm. Swearing's not so bad I don't think. You've just got to confess it to Father John and it's not a sin on your soul no more.

Good Lord, he said. Aren't you something else. Confessing to Father John. Who's ever heard of such a thing as thinking about confessions before misbehaving. Seems a bit backwards.

Swing turned toward the back of the truck.

Father John, our pastor and superintendent over at St. Mary's Elementary in Sleepy Eye where my sisters and I went to school, required regular Holy Reconciliation for us students like every day was the last day and we were all just moments away from death by rogue lightning bolts out of clear blue skies, paralyzing sickness spread by mosquitoes, fallen power lines sizzling across the yard, murder by a sleepwalking child who can't be waked to sense, dirty needles planted under gas pump handles by bitter homosexuals with AIDS, or God's plain old, unpredictable will at any moment. We had homilies about all of them. For both the regular Sunday and Wednesday school Mass, he'd flap his robe, point, and spit,

Take heed, the moment of death is always upon you. Every time you drive and meet a car on the road, you are four feet, just *four feet* from a head-on crash and fiery death. Are you ready? Is your soul ready? You will not, will not enter the kingdom of God with mortal sin on your soul. No. No. Have you coveted you neighbor's goods? His wife? Have you lusted, stolen, or hurt another with angry words? Have you disrespected your parents? Used God's holy name in vain, missed Holy Mass? You will not have time for the perfect confession, I assure you. Why chance eternal Hell when you could simply cleanse your black souls with confession and penance, Father John said.

Most of the time, though, I was so fresh with a recent confession that I had to make up sins to confess on the way from school over to church for Reconciliation so that Father John wouldn't get mad at me for not taking the sacrament seriously. I'd confess stealing from Mom and cheating on tests even if I never did it, which made me feel kind of bad, so I let myself swear pretty regularly just to keep some sins ready for Father John at confession time. It never earned me more than three or four Hail Marys and an Act of Contrition for penance anyway. Mom and Dad didn't say much about my swearing unless I'd let one slip in front of someone important, like the mailman or insurance guy.

I followed Swing to the back of the truck, talked at his back.

That's how everybody around here talks, I guess, I said to Swing.

Well if everybody jumped into the lake, would you jump too?

Don't know, Eddie, I said.

You call me Swing. Nicknames are for men, and I'm proud of mine. Got it for my batting average back in high school and for something else you're too young to understand.

Oh I know all about that sort of thing, I said. Pretty much everything there is to know, I bet.

You are something else, Miss Nicole. You get your ways from your momma or your daddy?

Both probably, I said. I knew I got my lank and dirt color from Dad's side and my expressions from Mom's.

That your momma out in the garden there? Swing asked. In the bikini top? Or your sister?

Mom's scowl and tight mouth never stopped men from looking at her. She was short and full and had bouncing hair full of curls that looked good brown or blond or red or whatever combination of those she wanted. Her whole body swayed like a windy treetop when she walked, and she wasn't wrinkled like my uncles' wives because she wore sunscreen and spread Oil of Olay on her face and Vitamin E around her eyes every night. And while she watched *The Price Is Right,* she stretched her legs and did sit-ups and only drank water even if we kids were drinking Kool-Aid. Sometimes when my sisters and I were in the bath, she'd turn her back to us, pull down her bra, and smooth Cocoa Butter over her breasts and we tried not to let her see us looking at her and wondering.

Damned stretch marks, she'd say. A woman's got to keep up her looks, girls. No sense in looking like something out of *National Geographic* at thirty years old.

Swing squinted at Mom bending over strawberries in the garden for a few seconds more. Mom wore her black swimsuit top, though she wasn't planning on swimming or running through the sprinkler with us girls. The summer had been dry. The Little Cottonwood River was dusty, and Dad said no to hooking up the sprinkler to the hose for cooling off or wetting the lawn.

That's Mom, I told him. And Dad's in the granary right over there, I added.

Swing laughed and stuck his green eyes on me again.

Ha, he said. Point taken. You're mean to your dogs and got a dirty mind besides. There must be something in the water out here. I been on this route only one day and am convinced of it. You're growing some very pretty things, but they're all mean as cockleburs underneath. You don't want to be mean now, do you? Be gentle like a good girl and take that crook out of your brow.

Swing reached out and tapped my forehead, the first boy ever to touch my face, even if he wasn't a boy really, even if he was probably twenty-five or more and I was only twelve. I decided it probably doesn't count if a boy who is more than ten years older than you touches your face.

Right here, he said holding his finger to my forehead, needs relaxing.

I backed up from him then, felt heat spread in my cheeks though I knew my face wouldn't give it away. My dark skin hid a blush.

I gotta go help my dad, I said. I'll see you later.

I want you to come down here and greet me with a nice smile tomorrow. None of this Miss Colie Crabby Face kicking and swearing at dogs, okay?

Okay, I said, and headed back to the granary where Dad shoveled corn into the auger. I heard the milk truck roar down the driveway, but I didn't look. I didn't want anyone to catch me gazing.

Did you get the dogs down? Dad yelled above the noise.

Yes, I got them down.

Did you tell him not to drive so goddamned reckless?

No, I didn't tell him that. I forgot.

Forgot? That's about typical of you. Well, be sure to keep your sisters clear of him tomorrow. Anybody gets hit, don't come crying to me.

Okay, then, I said. And I relaxed my forehead and smiled right at Dad.

Get to shoveling, he said. Quit smiling like a goddamned fool.

All afternoon I practiced unwrinkling my face as I scooped.

Some nights after Dad's bowling or baseball games and after the bar closed and while I pretended to be asleep, I heard Dad in the kitchen, with a couple of his brothers, neighbors, or buddies playing Sheephead at the table and laughing and drinking Hauensteins, and I heard men slapping Dad on the back and telling him how lucky he was to be able to look at my mom all day and touch her tits whenever he wanted and couldn't they just have a little peek as long as she was sleeping and would never know. And Dad would say, You have no idea how crazy that woman is or how she fumes out of her mind at any old time, but you go ahead and have a look but don't touch or I'll bust your ass, goddamn it. I imagine in her sleep Mom looked like a cherub and peaceful and beautiful with her curling hair and naked body, and I bet those men talked about what they saw for a long time.

And more than once I heard something like this.

Do I have to go over to Sletta's and drag him outta his goddamned bed? Dad said. Is that the only way we're gonna get the truth of it? I see what I see, Marie, and I'm no goddamned fool. You will not make a fool of me all over this town.

William, shhhh. For God's sakes, the girls are sleeping.

But we weren't sleeping, really. In the moonlight, I could see Annie Jo's eyes pressed tight, but I knew she was awake because her breaths came light from her spot in the bed. We both listened, but we didn't say anything.

Well, get 'em up, he said. Maybe they should know what kind of a whore their mother is.

You son of a bitch. Don't you call me a whore when you've

got that tramp down at the City Limits and Suzie Klamp besides. I can't even go to church without seeing your women.

Oh my. You've got it bad, don't you? I gave you everything. You wouldn't have anything if it weren't for me. Nothing. And you repay me with screwin' my best friend?

What in God's name are you talking about? Who are you talking about? You're crazy.

Harry. Harry Sletta. It's all over town, and the girls said he was over here when I was gone.

What? So what? Neighbors stop by all the time.

Yeah. But he only stops when he knows I'm gone.

You're crazy. He's married, and he's your friend.

Well, he's talking all over town about you. About what an easy lay you are and how you shake your tits for him, you tramp. You just remember this. I say the word and you are out with nothing. Not a penny, an acre, and not the girls. Nothing. I gave you everything.

The hall light shone under our bedroom door, lit the room to gray.

Annie Jo's eyes broke open, scared me to a gasp.

Colie, she whispered.

Go to bed, I said. And I turned over.

Harry Sletta played baseball with Dad. He bowled with him in the winter, too. Dad got over worrying about Harry and Mom enough to keep bowling with him and drinking after. The team had on it Lester Haus, Bugsy Haler, Harry Sletta, and Dad. But Harry got himself killed in an accident one night when the car missed a single-lane bridge approach and dropped down into a river ravine a couple miles north of our house. The phone rang and rang the next morning, and Dad wouldn't let anyone answer it but himself and wouldn't tell what happened other than saying Harry was dead. Dad looked out the front window toward Harry's farm and held his head and cried all day. We girls opened our bedroom doors just a crack and watched. Dad had never cried before. And when Mom tried to ask him about what happened he told her to shut her mouth. When Mom picked up the phone to get the details from the neighbors, Dad said to hang up that goddamned phone. He said that we take care of our own out here and she better not be on the horn spreading dirt to anyone, either. What goes on at home, stays at home. Mom nodded like she understood what he meant.

Dad kept a framed picture in our living room of Harry, Bugsy, Lester, and himself leaning on rifles in front of three antlered deer that they shot on a hunt. He took care of Harry's herd until his wife could get them sold at auction. Years later, when Dad left us for good, that picture was the only thing he took with him.

Even after Harry was gone, Dad still worried about Mom. And it probably felt natural for him to start worrying about me. That's why Dad said I had my ma in me. He was always talking about her getting chased or her chasing someone else and was probably bothered already about me chasing, too, even if I didn't look much like Mom except for that crook in my brow.

Week later, Dad and I were grinding feed in the granary again when Swing pulled in. I had run down there every day of the past week to meet him and practice my smiling, though I told my sisters and Dad and Mom that I was just going there to call down the dogs so he could get his business of emptying the bulk tank done.

What the hell, Dad said. It's a wonder that milk doesn't churn to butter, the way he drives.

Dad shoveled another scoop of corn into the racket of the auger, shook his head, and laughed at his own joke—milk churning to butter. I stopped shoveling the corn into the auger to give Dad the smile I'd been practicing for the milk-man. He didn't seem to notice it.

A couple more scoops, he said and nodded to me. Then you go tell him to slow down.

After two more dumps of corn, I dropped the shovel too close to the PTO shaft, and Dad grabbed it quick before it mangled.

Come on now, he yelled, goddamn it. Use your sense.

I stopped, but didn't turn around to face him.

You're too young to be chasin' after a man already. Courtin' the milkman? Have a little shame. You've got your ma in you alright. Lord help me.

Yes, sir, I said to Dad.

But I ran off shamelessly quick. Outside the granary I yelled to Natty to put down that cat and come on over here because I had something to show her. She came, and I grabbed her hand. She brought the cat anyway.

Swing clamped the hose to the bulk tank in the milkroom and lifted his head when our shadows fell across him.

This is my sister Natty, I said to Swing. I take care of her and Annie Jo, too. I'm nice to them.

You treat her better than you treat them dogs, I hope, Swing said.

Oh I treat her real nice, I said. Don't I, Natty? Her name is Natalie really.

I gave her a little pat on the head, and she looked at me with raised eyebrows.

Watch ya' got there, Natalie?

Natalie lifted up her cat, Stumpy, for Swing to look at.

Well now, isn't this a pretty little kitten, Swing said. What happened to the tail?

Fell off, Natty said.

Nah, I said. It got caught in the gutter chain.

Oh, Swing said. Jeez. Can I hold her?

Yeah, but you got to hold her close, Natty said. She gets scared and shakes.

I'd probably be scared if I got my tail stuck in the gutter too, he said. I'll hold her tight.

Swing took the cat from Natty and held her to his chest all wet from the heat of the barn.

See? he said. She likes skin. Makes her feel safe and warm. He handed the kitten back to Natty.

C'mere Nicole. C'mere and let me show you something.

I left Natty's side and walked to Swing. Swing fingered my collarbone, said, Looks like you got a tree branch under here—don't you get enough to eat? You're never gonna fill out if you don't eat. Men like a little meat on the bone. Then he pulled my T-shirt and told me to tie a knot in the bottom.

I don't know how, I said.

Well, watch and learn.

He knelt and gathered my shirt in a tail, twisted, and pulled until a nice tight knot cinched the waist.

Give me that cat, Natalie, he said.

She handed it to him because she always listened to men and would have likely climbed right into the belly of the combine if a man, stranger or no, told her to. Swing reached his hand in my shirt, let go of the cat, and took his hand out real slow.

There, he said. He patted the kitten through my shirt. Now she feels safe.

I supported the bundle from the outside with my hands making a cradle.

See what a nice girl you can be? Swing said. You're a regular young lady with a little one there and child at your side. And no more crinkles in the brow. You don't need to look so old. Smooth forehead. Now give me a smile.

And I did. I saw my reflection in the steel of the bulk tank, which magnified my smile to take up most of my face, and it made me laugh.

When Natty and I got back to the house, Mom stood at the kitchen sink, cutting stems off strawberries. She nodded toward the milkroom where Swing climbed into his truck, pulled it into gear. She pointed toward him with her paring knife.

What're you doing down in that milkroom? Mom asked. Bothering that boy? You stay away from him. And fix your shirt. I don't want you runnin' around here like a little tramp. He don't need little girls bothering him.

I told her I was keeping down the dogs and that I'm not so little.

Mom turned quick, pointed that paring knife right at my nose. Don't you sass me.

I left Natty in the kitchen, went to the bathroom, closed the door soft behind me. I pulled a Vitamin E capsule from Mom's brown bottle, broke it and spread it around my eyes until they glistened back at me from the mirror. I pulled the knot from my shirt and slipped the entire thing over my head and tossed it to the floor. Then I took Mom's bikini top from the door knob, put my arms through the straps, reached behind my back and hooked it easy. The cups fell flat against my chest in wrinkled lines and I said, Damn stretch marks, to myself in the mirror. I pulled it off and pumped a glob of Cocoa Butter onto my palm, warmed it in my hands, and began working it over my breasts, hard nipples with just the beginnings of mounds filling beneath them. I thought about how Swing's hand felt between them until Annie Jo pounded on the door and said she had to potty.

Hold your horses, you little tramp, I told her through the door.

Next day, Swing pulled that milk truck into our driveway and kicked up the dust again. Mom and Annie Jo and Natty and I covered our bodies over the baskets of wet laundry we'd hauled to the clothesline and the dogs got up, shook themselves awake, and started barking.

Damn that man, Mom said.

I'll go, I said. And I dropped my plastic basket of clothes on the grass.

I picked up little Snuffy and pet him between his ears. I waited for Swing to open the truck door and get down.

Hi Swing, I said, smiled.

Hi Nicole. How ya' doing?

Fine, I said. How are you?

Why I'm just fine, Miss Nicole. I must say, your manners are getting better every day. You're getting to be the kind of girl a guy like me'd take home to his mother.

I smiled large at that.

He was only about an inch or so taller than Mom, but his shirtless chest glowed with muscles and was hairless as one of Natty's baby birds she was always finding under the cottonwood stand and nursing back to health.

I'll help, I said. I put down Snuffy and walked to Swing's truck and pushed back the door that revealed the hose.

Thank you, ma'am. We make a good team. Don't you think?

Uh-huh, I said. Then I imagined myself sitting beside him in that milk truck on his daily route and waving to all the neighbors who'd say, Hi Colie, nice weather we're having, isn't it? and me keeping down the dogs at old Moonshine's place or Dukey Kral's farm when we pulled in so that Swing could get his work done there without mutts threatening him with peeled back lips and shiny white teeth. I imagined Swing and me separating the whites from the colors together and choosing the best roasts from the butcher's selection together and reading the comics from the Sunday paper together and picking names out of the baby name book. I imagined myself a fine life.

Mom came prancing across the yard from the clothesline toward the barn, and I saw her before Swing did and my imagination stopped sharp. Her blue bikini top, the strapless one she wore sometimes to make sure she didn't get tan lines when she was working in the garden or hanging clothes, hung low, and her collar bones arrowed to the dark line between her breasts. And the white dishtowel she wore as a scarf contrasted her tan and her blue eyes shone, blue eyes that no one else in the family had, blue like the Little Cottonwood River after the winter thaw or a storm shadow creeping over an early moon. I saw her and wished she would turn around and head back to the house. She looked so beautiful.

I ached with that wish, but she was coming to talk to my milkman sure enough. Swing looked at me, then followed my stare to Mom, and he forgot to tell me to unwrinkle my brow and smile.

Rooted Here

**Jump-Roping Rhyme of
Sleepy Eye St. Mary's School Children**

Stay out of the haybarn,
her mother surely said.
You'll fall through
and end up dead.
D-E-A-D, D-E-A-D

Annie Mary didn't listen,
went up there anyway.
Fell through and hit her head,
was buried right away.
D-E-A-D, D-E-A-D

Her momma saw the ghost of Annie
walking here and there.

Her daddy dug her up,
saw she tore out her hair.
D-E-A-D, D-E-A-D

Poor Annie Mary,
screaming in her grave,
scratching at her coffin,
a dark and deadly cave.
D-E-A-D, D-E-A-D

Next to the little grave, an ash tree grows tall, but sparse, and drops dead branches. The soft wood of the trunk soaks into the stone of a four-foot wall, mortar cracked with age and wear. The petrified fusion of earth, wood, and granite hints that something between material and mystical occurs here. The memorial is the type of place where dandelions sprout thorns and tree bark runs horizontal. And, as it seems for all dwellings of the dead, the cool ground swells moss and releases a saturated scent. Mushrooms stroll along, and wild morning glories climb and clutch the field stones, hold them together in places, their tendrils like hundreds of tiny hands. No one harvests either.

Richard Twente built the wall around the grave to contain Annie Mary's roaming spirit. He plotted the trees, the stone fence, the grave marker, and his daughter's body on the highest hill of his farm site. He locked the iron gate, but she continues to stray from her resting place, and neighbors say they see her wandering over the hills, running her fingers over

wheat or alfalfa or dangling her feet into the Little Cottonwood River. Her skirt hangs heavy and dark. I saw her, they
say, saw her with my own eyes and you can laugh and call me
crazy but you just wait. Just wait until it's you seein' her ghost
and your blood runnin' cold with the sight.

Annie Mary's ghost parts her way through corn fields or
skips along the shoulder of County Road 22 as if it were still
field or gravel there and she still six years old and this era still
the 1880s. She looks for her daddy or her kittens. She was always chasing kittens. The foxtails, those long summertime
grasses that take over the ditches and lean toward the road as
if to pass gossip, sway with the swirl of her dress, and her long
hair whips in the wind. At night she cries because of the dark.
She never liked the dark. And to hear her is worse than seeing her. That's what the neighbors say.

The guilt of burying his daughter alive drove Richard
Twente to madness. He sold his farm to a neighbor, and it
eventually landed in the hands of a man named Fischer who
cleared the Twente homestead for crop land. He left only the
ash trees, the gated wall, and the headstone inside. The man
tended the site and told stories to his daughter Alvina about
the strange occurrences that brought the memorial to that
hill, stories about the little girl who lay underneath it all. Alvina married and had seven sons. One of those sons, William,
grew up, married, and had six daughters. One night in late
summer when his oldest was just eight, lightning struck one
of the trees growing next to the grave. Alvina called William
to come and remove it. He packed his ax and chain saw and

told his wife he would take the oldest daughter to help clear branches around the grave.

Put your shoes on, he said.

He was talking to me.

Annie Mary Twente died over one hundred and twenty years ago just down the road from my place. Grandma Alvina said she was playing in the hay loft of Twente's three-story barn chasing kittens when she fell through the opening and hit her head on the ground. The impact knocked her unconscious and slowed her breathing and heart rate. She was six. Her parents, Richard and Lizzie Twente, thought she was dead, had a funeral for her in a regular church and buried her in a regular cemetery, but, plagued by dreams and visions of the little girl wandering around the house and farm place over the next week, they insisted she wasn't dead and needed to be saved. Richard Twente dug up the body of Annie Mary. Her body proved she had been alive in her tomb, then suffocated. He then moved her to a plot on his farm place, south of Sleepy Eye, in southern Minnesota.

Had you been there the day Richard created the wall, you'd have felt a spring wind, sweet with lilac and brisk. You might've thought everything is waking in this land, everything is alive. The Little Cottonwood River runs strong, butterflies break from cocoons, irises push aside clumps of soil and stretch tall. You see a man digging a hole in ground freshly liberated of frost. A large mound of stones and a small headstone wait nearby, and you probably wonder at the irony of burying a child in a Minnesota spring. You wonder what trouble's rooted here.

Grandpa Leon and Grandma Alvina farmed the land around Annie Mary's grave. A rotation of corn and soybeans rooted, plumped, and died there every year, hid the wall and the trees in a shroud of sprouts, stalks, leaves, pods, and husks until fall when it all dried down and came out. Grandpa combined while Grandma stayed in the end rows with the grain truck and then drove it to the elevator or bin to empty, and I rode along. Grandma's was a waiting job. Stories poured from her in the lingering time.

> *Listen now*, she would say. *I'm going to tell you something. About that little girl restin' under that tree, the poor little angel. Look out the window there and think about this and be thankful to God that it isn't you scratchin' in the dark and being eaten by the worms. Now remember that this was before the days of doctors coming to look at every scrape and scratch you kids are always crying about, before the undertaker shot preservatives into the dead to keep them from smelling to high heaven, and before the steel coffins that keep the water from seeping in. There was none of that for Annie Mary Twente. And she was a beautiful child, head full of curls, like a porcelain angel. Suffocating all alone like that in the dark. Just six years old, imagine it.*

Had you been on the Twente farm the day Annie Mary fell from the haybarn, you might've said to her, Remember what your ma said now. Stay out of that haybarn. It's dangerous, child. You might have seen Annie Mary nevermind her mother, climb that ladder, frolick in the straw, and chase those kittens back and forth. Follow her up the ladder and watch her play. Every farm girl claims a corner of the loft where she sits and piles baby kittens onto her lap and rubs velvet ears between her fingers and traps the creatures under her blouse to feel their warmth, their life, and imagine herself full of it. Warmth and life. In a haybarn, you're always just missing things, seeing them out of the corner of your eye: might be mice or pigeons, barn swallows, cats, spiders, or straw dust, that release of dry wheat that enchants the air, cascades on it, tempts you to fly through it the way surface water bids you to dive. The haybarn's a nice place for loneliness and imagination. And maybe out of the corner of your eye you see Annie Mary there one moment and then gone the next. Maybe you hear a quick movement of air, a few pigeons take flight, and then you hear a dull thud and you feel a blunt tremor. Be still for a moment until the only thing moving is your own chest heaving. Tiptoe to the brink, the last place you saw her.

Look down from here. Look through the cut in the wood floor and see. Twenty, maybe thirty feet below, she seems poised for sleep. Her blue dress, faded from so many washings, looks like a nightgown from so far. She wears no shoes. Since it isn't Sunday or a school day and a six-year-old doesn't have much serious work to do, her hair hangs long and loose. It fans around her face. A strand covers one eye. Free straw particles descend from where your toe tickles the edge of the opening to where her body lays. Bend. Scoop a handful of the gold, open your hand over the hole and release it. Watch the sunlight catch the bits and set them on fire. See how they flicker and sink and christen the girl. Like water. Like handfuls of dirt. Like dust. Or ashes. And what but death could rest so peacefully? See how easy it is to believe her dead?

Richard Twente was a crazy fool, Grandma used to say, but when his wife, Lizzie, started having the visions too, the neighbors got worried. She was a good woman, my pa said, she wasn't prone to nonsense like her husband. Lizzie went half wild with grief, tearing at her hair and bugging her eyes, when Annie Mary fell through that opening. They had the funeral in the church with friends and family, and the pastor gave a sermon on how God sometimes calls the little children to bring laughter to heaven, but she still didn't feel right about it. Annie Mary's sister, her other daughter, felt peculiar, too. They both felt something was wrong, kept seeing the visions like I said.

If you had been there with Annie Mary in that black place, fetal and close and secure but cold, maybe you'd have felt her start to stir. Colors explode behind her lids, the colors of poppies and apples and straw and cantaloupe and leaves and

Monarchs and stars and sky. And yet, though the colors are so brilliant, she struggles to open her eyes. She doesn't know that it's black where she is, that there are no colors with open eyes. You see her lids fight against the sleepy weight. You hear the first mass of earth hit the top of the coffin. Breathe the fine dust that seeps through the cracks of the boards. She probably twitches her nose. She hears the thud and thinks it's the beating of her own heart. She wonders why she can hear her heart and why her eyes are so heavy. Another thud rouses her more and the colors disappear. Whatever dream had brought them is gone. Another thud. Another. Dust tickles her nose and she sneezes. Then swallows. Her lids still hang heavy over her eyes, but she's thinking. She tries to move a toe, a finger. And just barely, she scratches a firm surface, feels a sheet separating her from wood, it seems. She wants to open her mouth, but can't. Another thud and another. And, had you been there, you might have told her, Hurry! Before it's too late. Call to them. They could still hear you.

But she can't speak yet. Her body concentrates on breathing. And when the breaths finally come easier, which pumps the blood quicker, which sparks the brain that enlivens the nerves that twitch her fingers, her toes, and feeds her voice, the ground atop her is already six feet thick. It absorbs sound, stills vibrations, prevents oxygen from appeasing her lungs.

You might've told her to be still, to stop screaming, to not panic, that the air is limited. But Annie Mary's six. She only knows it's dark and cold and small and hard. She only knows to be terrified, and a child in terror cries and screams for her mother. You hope she'll pass out quickly, go into shock. But it takes a while. It takes several hours to exhaust the oxygen in that coffin. In those hours, she tears her shroud, she tears her hair, her face, gouges her lips, claws the coffin, rips at the wood. She's like an animal.

Twente went to that cemetery with a pick and shovel and started digging. A couple of neighbors went to watch, one by name of Haala and another by Fischer. They couldn't believe he was doing it, thought it was shameful disturbing the dead. Now Twente may've been strange, but he was a good carpenter and a decent farmer. Built that three-story barn and a granary with his two hands. Grew trees and vegetables galore. He was careful when he pulled those nails from the lid of the coffin. He knew not to upset it too much, or the whole coffin would cave right on top of that poor child, being it had been under the ground pressed by six feet of heavy, wet soil. No doubt he thought he should've made it himself. He pried the nails first on one side, slipped them into his shirt pocket, and then on the other. He slipped them into his pocket, too. He wasn't a wasteful man. The neighbors said he waited a bit. He was probably thinking about the sleeping look Annie Mary wore when he put her in there, probably hoped it'd still be there when he lifted the lid. He took a breath, they said, and lifted it off the coffin in one heave.

. . .

Or you might've been standing with Richard and Lizzie on top of that fresh grave. Follow them home. Richard swears he sees Annie Mary, hears her, feels her. Maybe you dismiss Richard's fidgeting, his wild claims, the way he screams at the invisible air. He's crazy, after all, and everybody knows it. But when Lizzie calls for her, your breath stalls. Annie? Annie, she says. Richard! She's here. There. By the well. Annie. Is that you, girl? Oh God have mercy on us. What have we done? My God, my God. What have we done?

Richard strides long and quick. Race to catch him. By the time you get to the cemetery, he's already pushed aside a foot of soil from her grave. Neighbors creep up, too. They whisper. Richard struggles to keep his balance down the hole. It's so cramped. Where to put a boot? A hand? Where to set this nail? There's no room to pry nails down there. He has to hoist her coffin above ground. And he does. Clumsily. And you think, that's no way to treat a person, dead or alive. But Richard's outside himself. He's enormously strong, not necessarily gentle. You've heard this about him before. He jumps from the hole, begins prying nails, putting them in his pocket. He digs his fingers under the lid at the head and begins to lift. The nails moan their resistance, tell him not to look. But that's what he's come for in any case. And that's why you're here.

The scream from Twente was something unnatural, Grandma said. *Annie Mary's eyes looked into his. He grabbed her little shoulders thinking she might be alive still. He shook her a bit and then brung her to his own chest. She was cold. He let her back down disgusted. But the guilt came quick. He grabbed and held her against him again. He rocked and wailed, threw his head back. Faced the sun and faced God. Haala vomited at the sight of it, the sight of a man cradling a corpse. Fischer went to Twente and forced his fingers open. Put her down now, he said. Put her down. She's all right now. It's in God's hands. It couldn't be helped. Put her down. Nobody could've known now, Richard. No one's to blame. Put her down. Leave her be. She's with God now. Put her down.*

Maybe you'd have stood there with Haala and Fischer. Maybe you went with them to tell their wives. See their disbelief, hear how they *do* blame. Of course they do. Sympathies wear quickly here, and soon the questions about Richard Twente begin. How could he not have known? Didn't he try the mirror test? Didn't he put it under her nose to look for breath? Surely, there must've been breath. He was a smart man. He could grow fruits and vegetables and trees and ward off disease in them, but he couldn't tell whether life was in his own child? It didn't make sense, they said. Remember that time he almost killed the whole lot of them? Drove his family like a madman over the hills in that sleigh on the coldest day of the year. His wife and children holding on for dear life. He was a strange man. Peculiar.

· · ·

Annie Mary's shroud, torn and crumpled, laid off to the side of her. She'd wrestled herself out of it. Her face was all marked up with scratches, she'd ripped out clumps of her own hair. Some of the strands floated right out of the coffin and twined around the hand of Fischer who shook them off like he was shaking off a spider. He said he always felt bad about that. Her nails were worn to the skin and had wood splinters and blond hairs stuck in the blood and thick of it. Her hands were cramped into claws. She had scratched at the lid of the coffin. It was full of gouges and blood and hair. Her face was frozen in white terror, red and brown with dried blood. Her eyes looked alive still, said Fischer. He said he was almost fooled himself when he looked in the eyes, but there was no doubt about it, she had suffocated in there after waking up from her coma. Richard Twente buried his daughter alive.

A terrible death lends itself to a restless existence, you'd have known. It's only natural the girl's spirit can't stay quiet, that she can't stop roving these hills and this river valley. And, like you, other people want to see her. Children ride their bikes down the gravel road to her grave and crawl upon the wall. They climb the tree. Take your sisters there, your best friend, Jenny. You and Jenny write poems here, prick your fingers with broken glass and press your prints into the wall. Scratch *Best Friends Forever* into the mortar. You pick ditch flowers and fashion bouquets for the dead girl. You leave barrettes, miniature Strawberry Shortcakes, fancy erasers that sit alongside the nickels, necklaces, shiny rocks, and other trinkets the little township girls of the past century have left for Annie Mary. The country boys leave bottle caps, bird bones, and urine streaks down her headstone. They bring her tale first to the Little Red Schoolhouse in Albin township, then to St. Mary's Grade School in Sleepy Eye. Some of the nuns grew up here, too. They know the story of Annie Mary Twente and threaten curious children with *Behave yourself now or Annie Mary'll be sure to grab you in your sleep and pull you down to the devil with her.* Mothers use her story, too. *Stay out of the haybarn,* they say. *Stay out of the haybarn or you'll fall through and end up thought dead and buried alive like Annie Mary.* But curiosity is stronger than the devil and stronger than the fear of falling. So the children continue to explore and continue to climb into the haybarns. They sing at recess time. *Stay out of the haybarn her mother surely said or you'll fall through and end up dead . . .*

Teenagers drink beer here. They throw bottles against the wall, climb the tree. You and Jenny swill blackberry brandy and Haunstein beer here. You plan how to escape from this town, these families, this religion, how to throw off the burdens that bind you to Sleepy Eye. You drink until the bravery is in you. You test your balance by walking the top of the wall. You summon, command Annie Mary's ghost to show itself. But you see nothing, only hear the wind crying through the tree and weeping through the grass. You carve names into the mortar and into the bark of the tree. You bring boyfriends here. You open your body to the first boy you love here, the one who says he loves you, too, parked under the branches of the ash, alongside the stone wall. Let him push your jeans past your knees, kiss your fingers, arms, neck, thighs, and breasts. At sixteen years old, this seems the most wonderful place in the world—with this boy cradled between your legs, his face lit blue from the dashboard, and plans for the future passing between you. Don't think about the girl's bones beneath you. She's not down there anyway. She's above you, in the tree. Her eyes are watching. You see her over this boy's bare shoulder. Her eyes look very much alive. You are unable to make a sound.

You remember back to a time when you were very small, when you were here helping your dad clear a fallen tree. You gathered branches and threw them in to the back of your dad's pickup. It was cold, you remember, and wet, but you didn't complain because there was no complaining that your dad would stand. Your dad's chain saw, then ax, chipped in the late summer night and you were glad for the noise. It broke your fear, comforted you. When all the branches were finally gathered and your dad said to wait in the truck, you did. You wrapped your arms around your body and looked up into the other tree, the one that remained. And there, on a low branch, sat a little girl, long hair, white dress, shoeless, black eyes. She looked to be close to your age. And she looked to be watching you. Your breath stopped and you wanted to cry for your dad, but couldn't and didn't. For a long time you stared at her, and she at you. Finally, you slipped slowly onto the floor of the cab and put your dad's jacket over your head.

> *And now she haunts here. This field, that river. I've seen her a dozen times. What's worse, though, is to hear her. God in heaven, her cry chills these old bones. Annie Mary's moaning is like nothing sacred, I tell you. Listen now, if you hear that cry, cover your ears and say twenty Hail Marys. Otherwise, she'll try to tempt you down in that grave with her. There's no use pitying her. What's done is done. What Richard Twente did to that poor child is a tragedy, but her ghost is something else. It's the devil's doing.*

After Richard Twente uncovered his daughter, the neighbors helped him rewrap her shroud and bring her home. His wife and other daughter cleaned her face and straightened her hair. No one else would touch the poor child. No one else wanted to see the terror of it. Only a mother could do it, only a sister. They repacked Annie Mary in a coffin and set her upright against the barn until Richard could dig a new grave. This time he chose a hill on his own farm place. He buried her again. He chipped a headstone. He hammered a wood fence, but the spirit of her slipped too easily through it. He heard her dress rustle and at night heard weeping; her childish voice shook his bones and his soul and his mind. He saw her at the well, in the field, and in the barn. He tore down the wooden fence and gathered granite field rocks from the acres around his place and tossed them in a pile. He mixed sand, water, and clay into a mortar and began building. Building and building the wall to keep the child's memory alive, to keep the child's spirit from wandering again. He planted ash trees there hoping the roots would reach down, wrap around, and keep the coffin closed, keep the earthly things from getting in, and keep Annie Mary's ghost from getting out again.

Vanity and the Immaculate Heart

(SUMMER 1988)

Stained Glass

Suppose rumors spread through stained glass,
paint a tale of a mother weeping, pleading
go see the healer, Mary.

Suppose tinted panes
hide truth in grains of
a dove, flame, spirit
until light shines through and catches her dress
and beneath imprisoned blues
you see a shepherd's cloak
and swaying grass
make the bed for virgin flesh
and hear again these desperate cries
her mother spoke, thrusting bits of gold

weeping, pleading,
go see the healer, Mary.

Suppose only the windows know
how soft,
he lay
her down.

JENNIFER WENDINGER

Jenny's mom calls my mom one summer afternoon, and before the receiver hits the cradle, Jenny and I are dressed and packed for a religious retreat weekend with the Sisters of Schoenstatt. The previous sixth-grade school year had been rough for Jenny's mom. Jenny had taken to blaspheming and swearing and not wanting to go to church on Sundays and writing smutty stories about the school counselor. Jenny drove her mom to the end of reason, and I suppose that having Jenny around all the livelong summer's days without any school-day reprieve got Jenny's mom to thinking about the nuns and the solace of a few days with Jenny out of her hair and in the care of people whose goal it was to edify young Catholic girls in the ways of the Immaculate Heart of Mary. That's what the brochure said anyway.

All right, then, Mom says into the phone. We'll see you there.

She puts her hand over the mouthpiece of the phone, turns to me, tells me to get my nose out of the refrigerator and to go pack a bag.

Why? I ask.

You're going to the sisters for a few days, she says to me. She takes her hand from the phone, says, Uh-huh, uh-huh, yeah.

The sisters. Our school crawls with them. Sisters of every sort. Black habits, white habits, blue habits, no habits, veiled, unveiled. Sisters round, curved, and fat as baptism founts, some thin, stiff, and skeletal as a crucifix, some tall and severe as stone pillars, and some squat and fiery as votive candles. There are sisters who teach, sisters who tutor, sisters who clean, and sisters who cook. Sisters who are cruel, pull our hair and tie us to chairs for being fidgety, and sisters who are kind, put band-aids on jump-roping scrapes and star stickers on perfect tests. The only common things among them are their ages, which seem to range somewhere between fifty and a hundred years old, and their bare faces. High foreheads, white skin, parched lips, lashless eyes, gray irises. As if God had dipped them all in almond bark and set them aside to dry like a pan of Christmas pretzels.

I'm not going, I say.

You're going, Mom says without covering the phone. Now move it.

I march to my room, find an old duffle bag and stuff it with underwear, jean shorts, tank tops, T-shirts, and flip-flops. I pack my curling iron, brush, barrettes, hair mousse, and the blush Mom had thrown away and that I had salvaged from the garbage. I grab a can of hair spray and tuck it in, too.

Don't forget your Easter dress, Mom yells up the stairs.

You're not going to be running around like a little hoochie before God and everybody. Not like the way you were running
around in front of that milkman.

I pack my Easter dress, a tan thing that tickles my ankles,
and check myself out in the mirror. I consider tying up my
T-shirt into a knot to bare my belly, but think better of it. Too
hoochie, for certain.

At St. Mary's Grade School, girls wear navy blue jumpers,
skirts, or slacks with white button-down shirts. Navy blue
sweaters are permissible in cold weather. No T-shirts, no
shorts, no polos, no sweatshirts, no jackets, no excess orna-
mentation. Blue is the universal Catholic symbol for Mary,
the Mother of God. Statues and paintings of her always have
her dressed in a blue gown. Whenever she appears to some
impoverished sheepherding kids from foreign countries,
she's always wearing blue, they say. A heavenly color for a
heavenly being. White is a symbol of chastity, a reminder that
God chose Mary because she was born free of original sin and
because she was a virgin when Jesus was conceived through
the power of the Holy Spirit and remained a virgin through-
out her life no matter what those heretics who claim that
the apostle James was Jesus' natural—not metaphorical—
brother say. Father John says that we girls are likely to spend
all our time comparing outfits and seducing boys with our
short skirts, vulgar colors, and tiny tops if left to our own de-
vices; therefore, the dress code is not only justified, it's necessary to prevent the corruption of the young men and

women of this school. You didn't see Mary running around with her body bared before the men and boys of Nazareth, taunting them with her naked arms and legs.

The boys here don't have a dress code. They can wear what they want so long as it doesn't have holes and doesn't smell too much like the farm. If you were to stand across the street from us at recess, you would see a parted ocean: darting boys of every color of fish against slow-moving girls, taking care not to muss themselves, of blue and white waves.

This is bullshit, says Jenny about the dress code. Jenny undrabs her clothes, puts color into them any way she can. Barrettes with green, red, and yellow ribbons scroll down to her shoulders. She rolls up her pant legs, wears plastic bangles, friendship bracelets, colored socks, pink shoes. She smacks on lip gloss and eye shadow in the restroom. She fashions fake nails out of Elmers glue and pastes them on the tips of her fingers. She streaks Crayola markers to different strands of her hair, leaves curls of rainbow in her yellow tresses. She tattoos herself with the point of a compass and a pen. If we St. Mary's girls are the sea, then she's a spill of holy chrism that won't mix.

Mom's still on the phone when I pass through the kitchen with my bag. Dad has his nose in the refrigerator. He looks up, snaps a beer, and asks where do I think I'm going?

To the nuns.

He takes a quick drink and says, You aren't going to come back one, are you?

I hope not.

Dad points at me with a finger from the hand around the can, says, Well, whatever you do, don't sign anything.

I won't, Dad.

Can't be too careful. Before you know it, you might have your whole goddamned life signed away to the Pope in Rome. It's all a big money-making scheme and don't you forget it.

I know, Dad.

He takes another drink and heads outside. Before he lets the screen door slam behind him, he calls over his shoulder to me.

And for Christ's sakes, don't tell them your last name. They'll know you've got land. Next thing you know, they'll be out here askin' me to put the whole convent in my god-damned will.

Okay, Dad.

Keep your mouth shut, he says. I've got enough trouble keepin' that priest out of my business. And tell your ma to get off the horn.

He lets the door bump shut and strides to the barn. He tips the can to the side, allows a stream of beer to fall into the waiting jaws of the dog.

Okay, Dad.

He doesn't turn around, but raises his hand a little. To wave good-bye, I think.

Vanity came to me in fourth grade and followed me into the summer, though Miss O'Malley, our fourth-grade teacher, said it's the most dastardly of the seven deadly sins. Miss O'Malley's frizzed red hair and freckles screamed homely most days and plain at best on Mass days when she tied that mane into a ponytail and powdered her face a creamy puppet color. Mom said she could fix Miss O'Malley up into a regular beauty if she could just have half a day at the salon with her. A little mascara and blush would work wonders. Dad said it would be a waste of time—you can't cover ugly. Miss O'Malley was Irish, and I knew from my dad that the Irish are a different breed of Catholics altogether and can't be trusted entirely to interpret things quite right as they are the *following* sort and not the *thinking* sort. So he said. That seemed right to me. I didn't think God would choose seven deadly sins and set out one to be the worst among them. Deadly is deadly. There are no degrees to it.

Jenny said Miss O'Malley being ugly and personally opposed to pretty things was what made her say vanity was the worst of the seven deadly sins. And she probably heard that from her ugly red-headed mother before her. That's the way it goes, you know.

The Sisters of Schoenstatt built a grand retreat center and chapel on prime lakefront property—given to them by the diocese—for the enrichment, council, and education of young girls in the ways of Mary. The sisters themselves are called, they say, to be "another Mary," and they say our goal should be to live like Mary, too. Jenny wonders if that means we have to be virgins all our lives and if that's the case, the

Church is going to be in quite a pickle when the Catholic population drops to a big fat zero Catholics per a billion Lutherans and Protestants breeding like barn flies. I think this is a very good point but hope she doesn't make that argument to the nuns, who never take very kindly to being told their business. The sisters' navy blue habits swing around matte black boots, and their blue veils hide their hair lines so that we can never tell if their hair is gray, brown, black, white, or blond or if they even have any at all. A collar of white to symbolize their vow of virginity and chastity circles their necks and a medallion of the Virgin Mary holding her son, Jesus, sits at the center of their throats as a reminder of the Immaculate Conception. All their names are Sister Mary something. Sister Mary Edna, Sister Mary Madeline, Sister Mary Audrey, Sister Mary Clare.

When we get to the retreat center, Mom barely stops the car before she presses a check into my palm made out to Shoenstatt on the Lake Retreat Center and pushes me out the door. The sisters wait in the foyer for the rest of the girls and me. Jenny is the last to show up. She's nearly always late because she has to shower and rewash her hair every time she goes somewhere, even if she just washed it in the morning. She can't fix it right unless it's wet, she says. The sisters examine our tan summer skin, our wild, unbound hair, our bare legs, our shiny lips, our red nails with their own tight lips and stern eyes. Most of us move our bags to our fronts, to cover as much exposed skin as we can. An air conditioner hums above us and forces icy air into the room. And I wish, then, that I had something to cover up with. There's one nun behind all the others whose face isn't wrinkled and whose mouth isn't set in a frown. She smiles at me.

In fourth grade, we studied the apparitions of Mary. Miss O'Malley explained and showed us videos on how the Virgin Mary appeared to people around the world to give them warnings, to stretch her long, white finger at the ground to point out where God wanted churches, chapels, and cathedrals built, to encourage them to pray the rosary, and to tell them secrets, horrible secrets neither she nor they can tell regular people, lest we all overreact and destroy the world with our hysteria. Sometimes she brought along her son, Jesus, to emphasize the point, and sometimes she exposed her heart, which was almost always on fire like in all the paintings. Miss O'Malley said the Virgin Mary said God wants us all to behave like good Catholics on our own account, without Him having to give us ultimatums every time He turns around. He wants to give us a chance; that's why, after all, He gave us free will. But if we don't shape up, His wrath will be quick and terrible, and He doesn't mean maybe. God is especially mad at Russia according to three poor kids from Fatima—Lucia, Francisco, and Jacinta—who saw Mary floating on a cloud in a grazing field. She said Russia better convert or wars will spread and nations will be annihilated and the Holy Father will be beside himself with grief. And to Bernadette, a poor girl from Lourdes, she said, "I am the Immaculate Conception and I want a chapel built right here next to this stream to honor me, and recite this prayer every day. *O my Jesus, forgive us our sins, save us from the fires of Hell, lead all souls to Heaven, especially those most in need of your mercy.* Before you knew it, the chapel was built and lame people were pouring in left and right to pray the prayer and get healed in the stream, but only if they were true believers and not just looking for an easy way out of their paralysis or illness. God knows who the real Catholics are. He can tell whether you mean business or not, said Miss O'Malley.

Miss O'Malley's never gonna get a husband with that attitude of hers, said Jenny. She talks like an old lady already. And she looks like one, too.

We memorized the apparitions that were recognized by the Church as true miracles for Miss O'Malley's religion tests. We learned that Church officials examine these events carefully to weed out the hoaxes from the actual apparitions or every whacko with an agenda will be claiming to see Mary, Jesus, and all the Communion of Saints in his cereal bowl, potato chips, or house siding.

When Mary began appearing monthly to a group of Yugoslavian kids in Medjugordje in the early 1980s, we took up a collection to send to the kids for their petitions. Father John told a homily on how the Catholics of that country are persecuted and how Catholic women suffer rape and torture including having cats stuffed up inside them and left to claw their way out. Though Dad sighed and hung his head before the presentation of the collection plates, he pulled out his wallet and produced a ten. Mom crooked her brow at him until he pulled out another ten. Mom was always crooking her brow until he put more in the collection plate since the end-of-the-year fiscal report, which listed what every single parishioner donated for the year, came out and reported that Mom and Dad had given less than all of Dad's brothers and their families.

We also took up a collection to fund a pilgrimage for Father John and some parishioners to go and visit Medjugordje. My aunt went, and when she came back, she stood before the entire congregation and claimed the chain of her rosary had changed from silver to gold. See? she said and held it up. It's gold now. A miracle. And later still, we funded a trip for one of the visionaries to come to our church and speak. He brought a translator to interpret for the parish what it is he was saying. I didn't care so much about what he was saying as what he looked like. He wasn't all that ugly, the way I expected. He had very black hair that hung over his bushy eyebrows into his eyes. I sat up tall and tried to get him to catch my eye, and I thought just maybe if he did, he'll fall in love with me and then tell the Virgin Mary to appear to me, too, so I could see if she's real or not. But he didn't catch my eye. Mostly he kept his head bowed and his hair in his eyes the entire time, like he was shy or embarrassed or scared or something. The next Sunday, Father John reported that in a small rectory room, the Virgin Mary came to the visionary, and though the other people in the room couldn't see her, they could tell something mysterious and miraculous was occurring. You could just feel it, Father John said. The air in the room was different.

For several weeks after the visionary's visit, the people of Sleepy Eye experienced small miracles. One woman claimed angels hovered above the football field while our team played beneath. Some students believed the Holy Eucharist changed colors during the transubstantiation at mass. Lonnie Sellner's neck lump, a thing he was sure was cancerous but hadn't taken the time to get checked out, disappeared completely. I, myself, prayed every night that the Virgin Mary would appear to me. I felt like the only one who hadn't had a miracle. I wanted to see her, experience her heavenly beauty. I wanted her to tell me secrets.

The sisters lead us to our rooms. In each room, two sets of bunk beds line the wall, two desks with a simple lamp lighting the room line the opposite wall. Between the desks, a door leads to a common bathroom to be shared with the other girls. Study Bibles lie on all our pillows. The room is as neat and orderly as you'd expect a nun's room to look. There's none of the mess and chaos a girl's room usually has. No little-sister toys on the floor, no nail polish stains on the carpet, no sticky layer of dried hairspray on the desk, no clothes hanging over the hamper, no half-peeled Barbie stickers on the window, no underwear draped on the door knob, no dolls with their limbs missing, no two-bites-gone, browning, molding apples in the back of the closet. I take a moment to smell the clean in the room. I think this wouldn't be all that bad a life.

Snap out of it, Jenny says.

Jenny and I take dibs on the top two bunks. Jenny tells Lynn and Tiffany, classmates of ours, that they can have the bottom. Jenny and I put our pillows head to head and begin spreading our brushes, shampoos, and barrettes over our common desk. I line mine up as neatly as I know how.

There'll be no boys here to impress, says Sister Mary Edna. Her gray eyes, heavy lids practically hanging over the irises entirely, stare at our products.

Oh, we know, says Jenny. We just like to look nice.

Sister Mary Clare, who looks a lot like the woman on the bottle of Mom's Oil of Olay, picks up Jenny's apple shampoo and flips open the top. She pulls it to her nose.

Smells nice, she says.

Thanks, Jenny says and takes the bottle back.

Time to prepare for lunch, Sister Mary Clare, says Sister Mary Edna. Sister Mary Edna stretches her arm toward the door. An invitation for Sister Mary Clare to get out.

Sister Mary Clare lifts her brows and says, Alright, and turns and squeezes her habit out the door. Sister Mary Edna follows, gives us one last glance before she closes our door.

Jeez. She's young, says Jenny. Poor thing.

Who? asks Tiffany.

Who do you think? says Jenny.

She looks kind of elegant, I say.

Sometimes I worry about you, Colie, says Jenny.

. . .

Jenny and I share her curling iron while we prepare for chapel. When I tell Jenny that I'm praying for a vision, she looks at my mirror reflection and says, Dream on. Look at the photographs. You've got to be ugly and poor to get a visit from the Virgin. That Lucia girl looks like she has a moustache. I'd rather be pretty than have a miracle. As soon as you have one, everyone expects you to become a nun. Who wants that?

Why do you think Sister Mary Clare is a nun? I ask.

Probably she just wanted to get away from her family and didn't know what she was getting into.

Yeah. Probably, I say. I pull my hair up into a barrette. Give the entire bunch a fluff.

Rat the back of my hair, would you? says Jenny.

I rat the back of her hair.

At chapel, Sister Mary Edna leads a litany to Mary. Sister Mary Edna, Sister Mary Audrey, and Sister Mary Clare kneel in the row ahead of Jenny and me. Their prayer hands rest on the banister in front of them, light and airy as patient moths. They keep their eyes closed, their chins tucked, their lips loose.

Please bow your head, says Sister Mary Edna. Holy Mary.

Pray for us, we respond.

This litany is robotic, so as I respond, I look around the little chapel of Shoenstatt. An afternoon sun lights up the stained glass windows, fires colors down on us. I think that this must be a nice place for the sisters to pray and let the reds and yellows and purples disregard their muted habits. Colors move in here. The sun rearranges Mary's glass image, makes her stir across the floor or along the pews. Her stained glass body always bows below the Angel Gabriel, bows below the cross, bows below her son, bows below the Holy Spirit in the dove, or bows below God. But her reflection seems to be running around, trying to get off its knees and move about freely.

Holy Mother of God,

PRAY FOR US.

Holy Virgin of virgins,

PRAY FOR US.

Mother of Christ,

PRAY FOR US.

Mother of Divine Grace,

PRAY FOR US.

Mother most pure,

PRAY FOR US.

Mother most chaste,

PRAY FOR US.

Mother undefiled,

PRAY FOR US.

Virgin most prudent,

PRAY FOR US.

Mirror of justice,

PRAY FOR US.

Seat of wisdom,

PRAY FOR US.

Queen of angels,

PRAY FOR US.

Queen of prophets,

PRAY FOR US.

Queen of confessors,
> PRAY FOR US.

Queen of virgins,
> PRAY FOR US.

Queen conceived without Original Sin,
> PRAY FOR US.

Queen of peace,
> PRAY FOR US.

Pray for us, O Holy Mother of God,
That we may be made worthy of the
promises of Christ.

The late summer sun stretches and pushes the window hues down the chapel walls and onto the floor. Reds, purples, and golds erupt in Jenny's hair, as if the Virgin Mary image had punched, shattered, and spilled the panes. Jenny picks red nail polish from her fingernails and brushes the flecks to the floor, leaves a scattering of tiny red drops on the marble tile.

When curfew sends us girls to our rooms, we dress in our pajamas and climb into bed. Jenny and I lean over the side and hang our heads over the edge to whisper with Tiffany and Lynn below us. Lynn twists and turns Tiffany's long blond hair into a thick braid.

Sister Mary Clare was a Sellner girl, Lynn says. She had the most beautiful hair, long brown curls and never even had a perm. Hold still, Tiffany. Just totally natural, you know?

Tiffany holds her head stiff.

I wonder if she still has it, Tiffany says. Do you think they make the sisters cut their hair? Or do you think it's just shoved under there?

They have to make them cut it, Jenny says. Otherwise it's vanity. Long hair is vain. They have to give up their hair just like they have to give up money and have to be virgins.

God, Lynn says, if I hear the word *virgin* one more time, I'm going to throw up.

Did you happen to notice that like every one of those litany titles was about Mary being chaste? We get it already.

Jenny and I laugh and snort the way we never did in front of boys.

You guys, Tiffany hisses, be quiet or we're going to get in trouble. Anyway, that doesn't make sense. Mary had long hair, and she's like the holiest woman ever. I'd never cut my hair to be a nun.

How do you know she had long hair? I ask.

All the paintings and statues show her with long hair, Tiffany says. Duh.

Well they show her with skin white as snow, too, I say, but that can't be right. She was dark as an Indian, I bet. Dark as me for sure.

Yeah, she says, but you're probably half African or just dirty maybe.

Very funny, I say.

Anyway, those kids who see her say her hair is long and that she's the most beautiful woman you can imagine, Tiffany says.

Lynn wraps a band around Tiffany's braid and tosses it over her shoulder.

There, Lynn says. All done. Yeah. Beauty is vain, so why isn't Mary committing a sin by being beautiful? And if she's not, then why can't sisters keep their hair?

Jesus Christ, I say, this is giving me a headache.

You've got to confess that, Tiffany says, that's taking the Lord's name in vain.

Whatever, Tiffany, I say. God.

Yeah, says Jenny, thanks, Mother Teresa. Maybe you want to hear confessions or take care of some lepers before bed.

I'm glad for Jenny's defense, but I already know that I will confess taking the Lord's name in vain, and I wonder if I shouldn't stop doing it altogether.

I push myself back onto my bed, lay my face on my pillow, and wonder what I'd have left to confess to Father John if I stopped swearing, and I decide he probably wouldn't believe me if I didn't confess swearing and taking the Lord's name in vain at Holy Reconciliation so I decide to keep doing it in moderation.

Whatever, Tiffany says.

Do you think the sisters sleep in their habits and veils? Jenny asks.

I don't know, Lynn says. Maybe you should go find out.

Yeah, Jenny says to Lynn. Maybe I should. Then maybe we can tell if Sister Mary Clare still has her hair. I'm gonna go say you're having your period and don't have any pads.

Gross, Lynn says. Even if I were, I wouldn't use nun pads.

They've probably been soaked in chrism or something, I say.

I bet when a nun gets her period she calls it the stigmata, Jenny says.

No shit, I say.

You guys are rotten, says Lynn. So, Jenny, are you gonna go or what?

Yeah, I'm going.

Jenny springs down from her bed, lands with a drop as soft as a sprinkle of Holy Water on Christmas Eve Mass and tip-toes to the door.

In fourth grade, rosary came right after lunch. Right after winter recess when your knees and legs ached and itched with the blood finding its way to them again. To do the rosary, you stood up, pushed in your chair, and knelt beside your desk even if your frozen limbs fought you. The cold linoleum floor bit your knobby knees. But you were grateful you weren't the Bertrand kid with scoliosis, the kid who leaned to one side so severely you feared he might topple and knock his noggin on your desk or, worse yet, fall into your lap. And you were grateful that this is the only time in the day you had to do this. It could've been worse. You could've been one of the Weichel kids whose parents required nightly after-supper rosaries besides the ones the kids did in school. Or you could've been the Stolks kid, the kid whose Mom wasn't Catholic. The kid who didn't know how to lead the rosary and stumbled over the *thees* and *thous* in Hail Mary and mixed the Before Meal Blessing into the Glory Be and for some reason put his right hand over his heart while he attempted the Apostles' Creed and despite all this still got chosen to stumble through it at least once every two weeks under the glare of every fourth grader with their knees taking turns bearing weight, under the glare of Miss O'Malley with her red hair alive like the Northern Lights, under the glare of Pope John Paul the Second with his stern glower frowning down from his photograph, under the glare of Jesus Christ on the Cross with his body bronzed and stiff and stretched and whipped and poked and nailed, and may God forgive you if you even thought about complaining about your pained knees and runny noses when there sat Jesus on the cross—dead for your sins, and under the gaze of the Virgin Mary herself, centered in the shrine dedicated to her. Arms extended, feet tangled in the serpent, and pious face fashioned in eternal, in sad—in dreadfully sad, sad disappointment. And no matter where you sat in the room, she seemed to be looking right at you.

When Jenny comes back, she's carrying a box of Fruit Loops.

Hey guys, the nuns are holding out on us, she says.

Hey, pass it around, says Lynn.

So? asks Tiffany.

So what? says Jenny.

Well, what did you see?

Ahhh. I just went to the kitchen. I didn't see anything, just a couple of nuns walking back from the chapel. Probably had a midnight service or something.

Or maybe a virgin sacrifice, I say. I toss a handful of cereal into my mouth.

Yeah, says Jenny, probably a virgin sacrifice. Come to think of it, I didn't see Sister Mary Clare. I bet they put her on the altar and commended her spirit to the devil.

We toss out images of Sister Mary Clare on the altar. Naked. Or clothed in leather. Or fastened at the wrists and ankles with snakes. Writhing around in pain. We say maybe she whips her hair around like all the movie stars do. We lie on our beds and imitate her. I flop my arm over my head. Lynn pulls her pajama skirt up high. Jenny crosses her arms over her breasts.

We snicker and snot until a tap rattles the door. We go silent, and I can hear my pulse in my ears.

Girls?

It's Sister Mary Clare, whispers Tiffany. We all look at one another, snap off the light, then climb under our covers.

Come in, says Jenny.

Sister Mary Clare, still dressed in her habit and veil and not letting on about whether she has hair or not, swishes through the door.

Girls. You're keeping up half the floor. Now get to bed before I send Sister Mary Edna on you.

We can't sleep, whines Tiffany.

And why, may I ask, might that be?

Because we're used to music at night.

Is that right? Interesting. So if I find you a radio, you'll go to sleep?

Absolutely.

Jenny, why don't you come with me. Let's go find you and your roommates a radio.

Uh . . . Okay, says Jenny.

Sister Mary Clare points to the Fruit Loops, sitting on Lynn's bed.

And give me a handful of those Fruit Loops.

Lynn hands over the box. Sister Mary Clare pushes up the sleeve of her dark habit and reveals a long, slender forearm, slips it into the box and pulls out a closed fist of colored cereal.

Let's go, she says. Then she picks a Fruit Loop from her palm and places it on the tip of her tongue.

On your fourth-grade knees, you removed your rosary from its velvet pouch. The sound of thirty kids pulling their beads from these purses simultaneously is something you would never forget, though you didn't know that then. It was the sound of a thousand Roman hammers on a thousand Roman nails piercing the skin, muscle, and bone of Jesus and breaking into the cross for each transgression you commited. *Every time you sin, another nail penetrates the hands and feet of Jesus. Every time you swear, you steal, you cheat, you masturbate, you fasten Jesus to that cross over and again with your wickedness.* The clacking of each redemptive bead signified each redemptive prayer, each petition you murmured for the next half hour to save yourself from the fiery flames of eternal damnation, to lift the souls of those limboed loved ones and forgotten ones into the warm embrace of Jesus in Heaven.

But all you wanted to think about was that you want a new rosary, one of red gems like Lisa or white pearl like Sarah or clear diamond like Jackie. You wanted to hide your black rosary. It's old and ugly, you thought. Black rosaries are for boys, you knew. But it was better than having to use your fingers like Alan, the poorest kid in fourth grade, whose pant legs left his raw, probably frost-bitten ankles bare and whose winter coat smelled like hay and bacon, but whose hand clutched a heavy collection envelope every Wednesday Mass day and whose family donated the pigs for the annual Church benefit dinner.

You held the beads between your fingers, began with the metal crucifix swinging at the end of the chain, made the sign of the cross with it, touched the metal to your forehead, your heart, your right shoulder, then left. Then kissed it. You recited the Apostles' Creed. *I believe in God* . . . Moved on to the first bead. An Our Father. Then three Hail Marys for faith, hope, and love, then a Glory Be. You let the prayer leader announce the first of the Joyful or Sorrowful or Glorious Mysteries. You meditated on the annunciation or the agony in the garden or the resurrection while you recited another Our Father, ten more Hail Marys, and another Glory Be. You started all over. Repeated four more times. When the rosary was complete, you delivered the Hail Holy Queen. You put your rosary back in its pouch. Got up off your knees. Rubbed the life back into your legs, but you were discreet, so as not to suggest you begrudged Jesus a little suffering on your part considering all He had done for you.

Later, at home, when you had your pant legs rolled to look at your purple and blue bruises in front of the TV, your dad asked who the hell capped your knees.

We did the rosary today.

Oh, he said.

Oh God, whispers Tiffany. We're dead. We're in big trouble.

Shut up, you retard, says Lynn.

I wonder what Sister Mary Clare wants with Jenny, I say. As if she really needs her to help find a radio.

No shit, says Lynn. Maybe she's been listening to us the whole time.

Maybe these rooms are bugged, says Tiffany.

Yeah, the Church's got connections to the mob, you know, says Lynn.

How do you know this kind of stuff? Tiffany asks.

My mom, says Lynn. She tells me everything.

On Fridays we didn't have meat at school lunch. The bishop said we were fasting for vocations. The bishop took boys from our class and brought them to a special prayer group once a week. He hoped to convert a boy or two to the priesthood. Kevin Busherd thought he might join up, said it was a pretty good deal. You get a house and a car and all your bills paid. You get a housekeeper and cook, too. And you've got travel and job security for the rest of your life. We girls speculated about which one among us might become a nun. Maybe Jane Zeitl, she was too fat to get a husband anyway, we said. Or maybe Christine Weisner, who liked to sit real close to us and pet all the girls in the class. Might've been Bobby Jo Domeier, she had no friends and could've used the company. Maybe Tanya Sellner, she played Mary in the Nativity play. Remember how seriously she took her part? How cool she thought she was? Or maybe you. It might be you. You always look real holy at rosary time. No way. Not me. I want to get married. I want kids. I don't want to be a virgin.

Jenny comes back alone. She doesn't say one word to us, though we've been waiting and thinking and wondering if she's been sent to go pray all night, or do some nun chores, or kiss the statue of Mary a thousand times. She brings a small radio, which she plugs in and tunes to 96.7 FM. Finally, she says Sister Mary Clare told her she listens to this station, says it has great tunes. The radio chimes in quietly; Def Leppard music surprises us.

What, no church music? says Tiffany.

Nuns don't just listen to church music, dumbass, Jenny says.

You spend ten minutes alone with a nun and all of a sudden you're an expert? says Tiffany.

Are you and the nun budding up? asks Lynn.

No, Jenny says, I'm just saying that she says it's a good station. It's not a big deal.

Jenny's gonna be a nun, I bet, says Tiffany.

Grow up.

Well, it sure sounds like it, says Tiffany.

Whatever.

Did you ask about her hair? I ask.

No, I didn't feel like it, and why don't you just get over it already. It's old.

Jenny climbs up into her bunk, puts her head opposite mine. Tiffany and Lynn bicker below us. They talk about the creepy painting of Mary in the chapel, how it was looking at them wherever they sat. They wondered whether it was painted that way or if it was another Mary miracle. Maybe somebody should call the bishop. Soon, heavy breathing thrums their sleep.

Nicole, Jenny whispers later.

What.

She has hair under there. She didn't have to cut it.

Oh.

She says I have a very "congenial" personality, too. That's cool, isn't it?

Yeah. It's cool.

We're both quiet after that, but I can practically hear Jenny spinning her rosary prayers in her head. I stare for a long time at the black ceiling and finally, too, pray myself to sleep.

Caterpillar Hunting

(SUMMER 1983)

Mom and we girls spent a lot of time at her parents' farm, just a quarter mile from ours. We walked or rode our bikes down County Road 22, or climbed into Mom's orange Monte Carlo and made it in thirty seconds flat. Together, Grandma and Mom cooked sauerkraut and dumplings or chicken soup and gossiped. Grandma Haala would tell Mom how she didn't like for Mom's youngest brother, Greg, to go out with the boys. They were bad news and meant him no good, used him to buy beer because he was twenty-one and most of them were still in high school. They sported with Greg's simple mind, got him to do things he wouldn't dream of doing on his own, she said. But Mom, the oldest of her seven siblings, thought it was fine for Greg to get out and do normal things.

It doesn't pay to draw attention to him being slow, she said. Not unless some place'll take him in for good. You've got to cut the ties at some point and let him loose. Can't take care of him forever. Can't worry about every little shittin' thing. He'll be fine.

Who taught you to talk that way? I never in all my life heard such a mouth like the one on you, Marie, Grandma said. She stopped rolling noodle dough.

Oh my, said Mom. She rolled her eyes. She sliced a straight line through the dough, took the noodle, draped it over the chair to dry. She sliced another, balled it up, and handed it to the baby for a toy.

What your problem is, continued Mom wagging the knife like a winded tree limb, is that you think you can help everybody. Some people just can't be helped, and it's better to let them go. Sink or swim for Greg. It's about time.

Says you, Grandma said. That's what you say. You don't care what I go through, what people say. No siree. It's nothing to you.

Oh my. You've got to learn to be satisfied with what you've got. You've got six other kids, old woman. Plenty of grandkids already, too, in case you haven't noticed it.

Greg's slow, Grandma Haala said. But not slow enough for anyone to be able to do anything about it, and Lord knows how I've tried to get him help over and above what any good mother should be expected to do. What else can I do?

Greg had a long-armed walk that anyone from a mile away could mark as that of a man not thinking quite straight, like he was paying too close attention to each step or his big toes were missing. Saliva clogged his mouth, too, made it hard for him to speak clearly. He drooled while he watched TV and spit at every hard consonant. People mostly stepped back from him while he talked, though kids sometimes said, *gross* or *that's disgusting*, but Grandma wouldn't let us talk that way to Greg. We knew to be nice and let him go on rambling.

Greg was useful to us in ways, though. He was an expert at helping my sisters and me trap new pets after distemper disease killed our cats or our dogs had gone down under the wheels of passing cars while they waited for the school bus that brought Annie Jo and me home from St. Mary's Grade School. The dogs never could wait patiently, always had to chase cars and nip at the wheels.

As a kindergartner waiting for the bus, I watched a white car with a blue top run over my dog, Softy, and drive off. I saw Softy tremble, shake, and try to pull and bite his body away from his leg, squashed and mashed into the road. I recognized that death flop years later, when Dad would let us shoot the barn swallows with our BB guns in the machine shed. Dad didn't like for the birds to mess his machinery with their droppings, so he let us practice our aim on them in the shed so long as we didn't pump our guns so hard that the BBs could pierce the metal and cause all sorts of spots and rust in the walls and ceiling. When we hit the birds good, they fell from the rafters and landed with a puff on the thin gravel floor. Their wings rolled back and forth and caused all sorts of commotion before either we shot them a few more times or the cats pounced on them and put them out of their misery. Softy was in the throes of that death flop when I ran back into the house crying so hard that I couldn't even see through the tears. I pointed out the window and said, Softy, to Mom. She looked, then told me to pull myself together, get back out there, and wait for the bus. She sent Dad and his friend Harry out to scrape Softy up; they put him in the back of Harry's pickup and turned back into our driveway where I stood waiting for the bus.

Shake it off, Dad said out the window.

They lay Softy under a cottonwood tree in the yard. The vet, on our place to clip the horns off the calves, came over and took a look. Said there was no use, though he'd try. He stitched up Softy's side, and tried to set his leg. I caught my bus and went to school. Softy died when I got home. I didn't cry then, and I never cried over a pet again.

Animals of every kind interesting to children—garter snakes, ring-tailed pheasants, opossums, farm cats, stray dogs, snapping turtles, field mice, gophers, and caterpillars—crawled from one ditch to the other over County Road 22, the new black strip that topped our driveway and led straight to Grandpa and Grandma Haala's farm. The road had progressed from walking path to field drive to gravel road to county highway over a couple decades, and what used to curve with the whim of the Little Cottonwood River was fixed straight with culverts and bridges and tarred with black and striped white and yellow by the Brown County Highway Department.

The ditch critters didn't know about the new tar road, didn't care if it was for cars, trucks, and semis. They kept their old breeding and water paths, and if those paths traversed over where the new road sat, well then they climbed right over. No holes, long grasses, itch weed, or county road threatened the prowl of Greg and my sisters and me when we were searching for new pets, either.

Greg taught us to play chicken with those semis, too. Chicken was when you'd see a semi in the distance and start circling your bike around and around on the road, circling a yellow line, dizzying your eyes and mind until it seemed a whirlpool of black and gold had opened up there in the tar and tempted to suck you down into a low world, just a pinpoint at the end of a spiral. You had to circle as many times as you could before the semi driver honked his horn at you. Get off the road and in the ditch before I flatten you, the horn meant. Greg was the bravest of all. He always took one more trip after the horn blared. Those fucking idiots can't get me, he always said. Goddamn idiots. He'd pedal hard and then lift both legs straight out into the air and then dive his too-small bike off onto the shoulder and down into the ditch. The semi, air brakes howling, would blaze by with a push of wind following its trailer. Pulses of heat waves would slap against my face and Annie Jo's face, would blow our hair and the ditch weeds wild.

Did you see that? Greg would say. That goddamned idiot couldn't get me. No siree.

Sometimes Grandma sent Greg down to our farm to get him out of her hair for a while because even though he was more than twenty-one, he was still a pest. Mom sent us all—Greg,

Annie Jo, Baby Natty, and me—outside so she could have a moment's peace in the house. Greg would leave us girls in the yard, then sneak away into Dad's machine shed. He liked the puff of diesel smoke that curled from the smoke stacks of Dad's tractors when they roared awake. He also liked Dad, admired him, copied him. So when he was supposed to be entertaining us, he would creep into the cabs of Dad's John Deeres. But Greg had the subtlety of a shot gun, and he shook the metal of the shed when he turned the key and pushed the throttle forward.

What is that fucking idiot up to now? Dad wanted to know when he heard the roar. Greg, he'd yell. You goddamned idiot, get out of that tractor right now. Goddamnit. I'm not running an idiot camp here. I've got work to do.

Dad threw the hose into the trough and climbed over the pasture fence, came running toward us girls in the yard.

Marie, Dad yelled to the house. He knew she was inside. Get your brother off my equipment.

Mom didn't open the door or push aside the curtain.

Colie, Dad said, you've got more sense than to let him in the machine shed. Use your sense, for Christ's sakes.

Mom came out then, picked up Natty, and walked to the shed. Annie Jo and I followed. Greg sat on the seat of Dad's 4010. He had the radio on and his hands on the wheels and his eyes straight ahead in some imagined field where he was the farmer who was towing the cultivator through the soybeans rows that hung heavy under the weight of their great pods, probably.

Greg, she yelled. Shut that off.

He snapped his face at us, and turned the key off. The tractor didn't shut down, just sputtered some.

Push in the choke, I said.

He looked to the tractor and pushed in the choke.

Then, except for a few barn swallows, the shed was quiet.

Greg, Mom said. Go find some caterpillars for the girls. Find them a bunch. Colie. Annie Jo. Go help.

Mom looked softly at Greg. She gave him an unlined face she hardly showed anyone. Then she turned and left the shed.

Greg climbed down from the tractor and followed Annie Jo and me outside. He grabbed his bike and climbed on. Annie Jo and I followed him down the driveway. He stood mostly, rather that sat, on his banana seat bike and stopped at the end of the gravel. He turned to us and said, Now, I only got room for one of yous. The other's got to wait here and wait her turn. Colie, get on here and you better not tip me over either. Annie Jo, you better not move and I don't mean maybe.

You're not the boss, Annie Jo said.

I am the boss. I am the goddamned boss. You call me Chief.

Chief is Dad's name, not yours.

When I'm the boss of you, I'm Chief.

I'm not calling him Chief. Are you Colie?

Sure, I said. Fine. He can be Chief for a while, can't he? Who cares?

Fine then, said Annie Jo. But he's not the real Chief.

Just be quiet and wait here, I said. We'll be right back.

I reached my leg over and balanced on the tip of the seat front.

We'll be right back, I said to Annie Jo. Stay off the road.

She sat down and started sorting stones.

Hang on, Greg said, and he pushed off and started pedaling. Pretty soon, Greg got the handle bars under control and we drove down the road steady. I held on and tried to make myself small and light and balanced as possible.

Shit, I said. I forgot to bring a container to put the caterpillars in.

No big deal, Greg said. You can hide 'em in your underwear.

Sure, I said. Quit spitting in my hair, please.

I kept my eyes ten to twenty feet ahead of the bike, looked for any movement on the road. I spotted a caterpillar a few yards ahead. A thick black one wrinkling its way across the tar.

Stop the bike, I said.

Okay. Okay.

I jumped off before he stopped and ran to capture the caterpillar. Greg waited on the bike. I picked up the creature with two fingers, put it in my palm. It curled into a ball.

Let me see, said Greg.

I walked over to the bike and showed him.

He's protecting himself, Greg said. See. Watch.

We waited a few seconds until the caterpillar stretched its body and began inching toward my wrist. Greg slapped his hand down just in front of its path. The caterpillar almost tipped off my palm.

Don't, I yelled.

Shut up, he said. Look. It curled up again. That way it can roll away from danger. Tuck and roll, just like motorcycle drivers on TV. The old tuck and roll trick'll save your neck.

Greg was right. The caterpillar curled tight, pulled its legs all together and stretched the fur on its back into an arch.

Let's go, he said. I closed my fist over the caterpillar but didn't squeeze, left enough room for it to move about but not escape. Greg helped me back onto the bike, and we turned toward home.

A semi, hazy in the summer heat, appeared on the horizon.

No, I said. Don't even think about it.

Oh I won't, you big chicken. What's your problem? Why you such a big baby anyway?

As soon as he finished speaking, he turned the handlebar slightly and began circling on the road. Round and round a yellow line.

Knock it off, Greg. I can't hold on with one hand.

Just hold on, he said. Those goddamned idiots can't get me.

Greg.

They can't get us.

The wind blew down the semi's smell before its sound. The sweet manure scent of pigs coiled around us.

Come on, Greg. Those pigs'll get squished to death.

What I knew was that those pigs were someone's liveli-hood, and that if that driver had to brake fast for us, they'd all be squashed and killed, and someone'd have to pay for that. I didn't want it to be me. I didn't want to make Dad mad.

Greg kept circling. The sound of the engine came then, and the driver must've made out our form because the long noise of a horn cracked the late summer afternoon. I jumped off the bike, got my footing, and scrambled into the ditch with my fist still closed loose over the caterpillar.

Come on, Greg, I yelled. Get off the road.

My leap had shaken Greg's balance, but he managed one more round before he lifted his legs, glided to the shoulder and aimed the bike toward me in the ditch. He plopped off the tar and onto the gravel shoulder, lost control, and flew headfirst over the handlebars. He crossed his arms over his head and somersaulted into the ditch near where I waited. The semi whizzed by us, whistled air, and hundreds of pig snouts poked through the slats of the trailer, grinned at us in the ditch. Greg looked up then and shouted hello to the sows.

Jesus Christ, Greg, I said. What is wrong with you? You can't do that. Mom'll kill me if you get knocked dead out here.

Oh we're just having a little fun with that goddamned idiot, he said. Don't get your panties all bunched up in knots.

Shut up, Greg.

I'm telling, he said.

Fine, I said.

In my palm, the caterpillar rolled about.

Greg stood and dusted the foxtails and seeds from his clothes.

Well, he said, let's head back. It's Annie Jo's turn.

No, I said. One's enough. One caterpillar is enough for all of us to share.

Suit yourself, he said. Get on.

Back home, Annie Jo and I asked Mom to poke fork holes in the top of a jar, and we filled the jar with sticks, leaves, and grass, all the things our little minds could imagine a caterpillar needing. Usually we forgot about the jars after a while. I don't think we ever saw one caterpillar through to cocoon and butterfly. It was that way with most of the animals we found. We used them, played with them, studied them for a bit, and then we threw them out when we were done. I never felt bad when they ran away or died. They melted back into the grass or into the soil, I knew. And I knew that dead things were necessary for living things, that living things depended upon dead things. I saw this every day.

Later that summer, Greg ran the loader tractor into the machine shed and ripped a big gash down the side of it that eventually invited rust and corrosion.

That retard is always one step away from disaster, Dad said. He sent Greg back home to Grandma and told him not to come back for a long while.

It's a wonder he's made it to twenty-one. I ought to put him out of his misery before he does some real damage. He's gonna get himself killed one of these days.

The Summer of Ordinary Ways

(SUMMER 1982)

I nestled under the kitchen table to think about the way of things and read and write notes and spy by pulling the hem of the tablecloth up a bit. I didn't so much as chirp a sound when I wanted to be alone. Annie Jo didn't think to look for me under there, wasn't old enough to dream up good hiding spots, so she couldn't bother me about helping her squeeze the pants onto her Barbie or playing school where she always wanted to be teacher and have me the student. And if Mom knew I was nesting under her kitchen table, she didn't let on. She liked to lock herself away often enough, too, and understood about privacy, and said she needed a little of it every day to keep her sanity.

The screen door slammed when Mom came in from the garden. A pup, trying to slip in the kitchen, caught his tail in the slam. He yelped like a bird, and Mom opened the door again to let him loose. She kicked the whiner away and yelled across the yard to Dad. Shoot them puppies quick, she said, before they drive me altogether crazy and I decide to dig a hole to Hell and throw myself, headfirst, down into it.

Settle down, woman, Dad yelled back.

Don't I have enough to do with the girls and garden and cooking and cleaning and picking up after everybody's mess and being nauseous day in and day out because of the baby filling up my stomach?

Mom always complained about the weight of the baby, how it pushed on her bladder and squashed her lungs. Her big middle made a labor of pulling laundry out of the dryer or grabbing the roast out of the oven. Once she said she may as well leave her head in there, breathe in the fumes, and deliver the baby unconscious. Be a lot easier that way.

I imagined Dad standing in the yard with his hands on his hips, dogs dancing around his ankles. He probably looked at Mom and shook his head. When Mom got in her moods, it was tough to know how to respond, and he didn't know any better than Annie Jo and me. Sometimes he yelled, sometimes he swore, sometimes he threw things, sometimes he slammed doors, sometimes he clicked the TV up as loud as it would go, sometimes he drove off to town, and sometimes he just paused quiet until the mood passed over her. When Mom intended to make a point, silence was usually best until she wore herself out of screeching and the red left her face.

I can't be bothered with a pack of thirteen useless mutts, she yelled. Always underfoot. Ugly besides. Bash them or drown them or shoot them. I don't care. Just get rid of them.

I refolded a worn note from Jenny, stuck it in my shoe, and scrambled out from under the table to help shoo the pups off the porch.

Mom called after me to get them dogs out of her sight. They make her sick and she's liable to puke if she spots one more ratty dog tail.

Dad shot the puppies in the milkroom of the dairy barn. I sat on the gravel outside the barn door, legs stretched long, picking the dead scab on my elbow. Annie Jo chewed a tomato on the cottonwood stump near Mom's garden, legs crossed Indian-style. She palmed and ate it like an apple and red juice slipped down her chin and onto her chest, shirtless and bony like a little boy's. When I tucked my knees into a chin rest, the waves of my shorts wrinkled around my hips, gravel grains clung to the backs of my thighs and calves. I wiped them off and passed my fingers over the dips they left in my skin. Grasshoppers sparked around me on the dry barnyard grass. It was that time in the belly of summer when grasshoppers come thick. One tangled in my hair just as the first shell popped from the .410 shotgun and the noise squeezed my lungs, took my air. I unwound the struggling grasshopper from a curl and heard Dad release and reload the gun. The remaining puppies yipped and scurried. Their nails tip-tapped the concrete under the echo of the shot and the barks. I pinched the grasshopper between my thumb and finger, and a runny mess dripped even as its legs still twitched. A second shot. More yipping and tapping from the puppies.

Mom stood up straight in the garden, rested her hand on the low curve of her back and pushed her stomach toward the hot sky, stretched her belly to God. She moved that hand over her brow and squinted toward the barn, told me to come away from there and took to hoeing between the tomato plants again. I threw the grasshopper into the grass and wiped its mucus over my scab. Annie Jo tossed the tomato aside and mopped her mouth with an arm. Tears leaked a dirty smear down.

Milly, the mother of the puppies, scratched under the granary door and tried to tunnel herself out, but a dog's paws and nails weren't made for digging gravel. She made little headway. She sniffed out, and puffs of dust smoked from there. Dad locked her in before we rounded up her brood into the milkroom. There were thirteen in all. Dad got Milly from his brother, Uncle Sue. She was a handsome black lab with a shiny coat and pink gums. Last April, Milly wandered and stayed gone a few days. I cried at school, told Jenny my dog was gone, and she said not to worry, that sometimes dogs get into heat and have to go visiting. Jenny knew about things like that. Our neighbor called after chores one night to tell Dad he had Milly tied to a cow stanchion in his barn because she was running with his German shepherd. Milly hopped easy into the back of the pickup, and Annie Jo and I climbed in the bed of the Ford with her and we drove home, the night-cooled metal of the truck pricking our bottoms, our legs, goosebumping our arms, twenty miles per hour only down the neighbor's half-mile driveway lit by a moth-busy yard light, past a soybean field leaned over with pods and a drainage ditch where coons washed their loot, onto County Road 22. The road, recently tarred, mingled with diesel fuel for two dark miles until we hit the driveway staccatoed with walnut trees on either side, our driveway. Annie Jo stroked Milly's coat and tickled her ears until her tongue slid down her jowl.

Back home, when Annie Jo and I rubbed the strain out of Mom's back and brushed her hair shiny, Mom agreed to let Milly sleep in the house, in our room. Annie Jo didn't want her to run away again. Mom said if she pissed in our bed, we'd have to clean the mess but it was okay with her otherwise. Mom's third pregnancy battled her. She'd lost a baby before me, and her eyes, layered blue, green, gray, and black—colored like the feathers of a blackbird up close—looked darkly on most things and hung low and slit small so that her face appeared hurt by a bright light all the time.

Jenny said that's how some moms get to looking after a while because it's a serious business being a wife and mother, keeping the kids and the husband on the straight and narrow, and not all women are made for it no matter what the Bible says. Jenny read her aunt's *Cosmopolitan* and made easy friends with the older girls on the school bus.

Bouts of gloom and wickedness came down on Mom with changing seasons or moons or pregnancies or baby stages. It started before she birthed me, I heard, after the first dead baby, and I heard, too, that melancholy and madness dripped like sap down Mom's family line, sticking every so often to one generation or another and sometimes pooling on one family. Years of conceiving, growing, and expelling babies labored her mind. And when the babies were birthed, their being out wasn't all that much easier on her. The babies cried and wet and got hungry and cried some more for no reason that Mom could ever figure out, though she would rock, walk, feed, change, swing, and bounce those babies all day and night. When nothing worked, Mom put the baby on the floor in the living room and sat and stared out the afternoon window, watched the seldom cars drive by on County Road 22. Maybe she wondered where they were going. Her skin broke out in red splotches and hair melded into three or four oiled strands and the nightgown she wore all day smelled of formula and dead skin and sweat and she stayed that way all week until Saturday night when she soaked in the bathtub two hours in water so hot steam poured from under the old, creaky door that she would not open no matter how bad we kids had to go to the bathroom. Maybe she soaked away pain, maybe old hopes or memories. Maybe she just soaked away the dirt, filth, and smell of mothering in preparation for church on Sunday morning when she'd be fresh and smiling for a while. Mom's mood shifted like the pattern of tree bark. Up close, the swirling lines and designs spin dizzy, but from afar, the trunk just looks brown and plain and quiet and beautiful. That's the way it was with Mom.

Mom flipped on a face for church that we hardly saw at home, one that invited smiles or nods or caused men's eyes to slide sideways and follow her. When Dad was good, he could tug that soft face out of Mom, and then we daughters would gather round the two of them even though what was happening wasn't ours to be involved in or to understand. Even though Dad and Mom ignored us in these times, it made me breathe easy just to be underneath their jokes and grins.

Dad warned us against making mischief around Mom. He said, Don't plague your ma, we have to make things easy for her so she can bring you a little brother to play with.

Annie Jo and I tried to be careful even if we had our hearts set on a sister and not a brother, but neither of us mentioned that little-girl wish to Dad whose dark eyes looked hopeful at Mom's belly even though everybody knew it wasn't decent to stare at a woman's condition no matter how big and round that condition was. Dad was certain he'd get a son this time, said the odds favored a boy as long as Mom stayed steady enough to build him strong and hold him firm until he was all ready and not let him drop through too soon like she did with the first baby, Dad's boy. So Annie Jo and I clipped our fingernails and dug out the dirt with a toothpick before Sunday Mass so people wouldn't think we were grubby during the peace-be-with-you handshaking time. We didn't cry or moan when Mom worked straight the knots underneath our hair, we ate Sunday salmon loaf without twisting up our faces, and we ducked out of her way when she looked ferocious, forehead crinkled and jaw taut. Annie Jo sometimes brought her a glass of cold milk or ice water while she watched *Guiding Light,* her favorite, and that was when Annie Jo and I would make small requests, while Mom was distracted with the going-ons of Phillip Spaulding and Beth Chamberlain or Josh Lewis and Reva Shane. Annie Jo had a round face that wrinkled easy with disappointment and deep eyes that welled up over the butchering of a buck or the selling of a steer. She's only four—she'll learn, Mom said.

Those Haalas are all nuts, Dad said. What we have here is a classic case of lunacy passed on from one to the next. Lunatics.

Mom's Uncle Eddie was off in the asylum over in St. Peter, her cousin Kathy was only let out of the home for short visits at Christmas, and her brother Greg, though he got old enough to move out and on, never could. Greg's state was caused by Grandma taking too many diet pills while she was pregnant with him, Mom said to Annie Jo and me, and Greg couldn't help the way he acted and the mess he made of everything and your dad shouldn't call Greg a fucking retard dumber than a box of rocks in a stone pile even if he did drive the loader tractor straight into the new machine shed and tear a hole in the metal. Your dad's yelling makes him nervous. It's just his nerves.

No, Dad said when we told him what Mom said, make no mistake about this, diet pills or nerves or no, a lunatic's a lunatic.

Mom's brother Jay, who lived nearby, never came around much, though we saw him through the car window when we drove by his house in Sleepy Eye. We waved and Mom honked the horn, but he would just nod his head from his picnic bench. That's where he always sat to drink Old Style. At Christmas or Easter, he broke into fits of laughter sometimes. Laughter that made you check to see if your fly was down or your underwear showing.

There's a crazy gene on your Mom's side, Dad said to us girls. Mom locked him out of the house when he didn't come home from bowling, and she sent Annie Jo and me out to the barn to ask him what he wanted for dinner. Annie Jo and I tried to shame Dad with severe eyes, pursed lips, and clipped words we learned from Mom. Dad said not to pull that shit on him. He wouldn't have his daughters telling him how to do his business or when to come home, either. This is my house, he said, and I'm king of it.

Dad drew a brown medicine bottle from the refrigerator in the milkroom, medicine meant for the calves, opened it, and twisted out a pill with a finger. He popped it into his mouth, washed it down with a beer. When the ache in his head stopped, Dad tipped over a five-gallon pail, scratched the dogs' bellies, and told stories.

Your Mom's family is crazy as goddamned loons. Don't ask me what's wrong with Greg. Who the hell knows. They can't get rid of him, though. He just keeps comin' back and that's good for those Haalas. Eddie thought he heard voices and saw bugs everywhere. The old man and old woman hauled him off to the mental institution in St. Peter. They left him there, pretended he didn't exist after that. Can you believe that shit? That's the Haalas for you. You get to be too much to handle, too much of an embarrassment, and they'll cut the ties. And your Mom's cousin? Loretta's boy? He hung himself. That was no accident. What kind of a stupid asshole *accidentally* hangs himself in the haybarn? That boy jumped from the rafters to get Loretta off his back. He put that rope around his neck and jumped. And all those Haalas sit around and talk like it was some goddamned accident.

What Dad said was true. I'd heard about it long before. I knew, too, that sometimes pairs of men talked sense when women bustled about changing diapers or cooking and weren't liable to overhear and take to frantics or shush the men up with sharp looks that could goosebump a neck or freeze an ear. But men don't know how kids hear and remember things, and men sometimes say and do things in front of kids that they shouldn't.

Wasn't heavy enough to hang himself, said my grandpa. *Must've snapped his neck at the jump.*

Yep. Looked like it, said my uncle. *We got him down from there before Loretta could see. She doted on that boy day and night. She took it hard enough I guess without seein' him swingin' there.*

Might be better off anyway. Ain't much of a life for a boy with his ways. Still though, Loretta's gonna take it hard.

Yep. She doted on him alright.

Accident, my ass, Dad went on. Those Haala women drive their men to death. Everybody knows it. I shoulda listened when Ma said not to marry a Haala. All they care

about is looking good to people. They've got no family loyalty. The Helgets have got loyalty and don't you girls forget
it. Think about who's here to help with baling and milking.
Who gave you this house? Who gave you this farm? It wasn't
the goddamned Haalas. I can tell you that much. Don't you
count on your ma's side. Those Haalas could care less and
are crazy to boot. They'd just as soon shoot you as invite you
for supper. A dog's got more sense for her pups. Just look at
Eddie. That poor crazy bastard. Inbreeding. That's where
that comes from. You rely on me. Your mom doesn't know a
goddamned thing about family loyalty. You'll see. You just
wait and see.

Dad got up, and the dogs scattered beneath him.

Ha, that's funny, Jenny said when I told her about Dad's story.
He's right, too. Except sometimes the women drive their men
to other *men*. Do you know what I mean? I bet you don't. It's
a big sin. But men on the Haala side sometimes get the hots
for other men.

Jenny was my relation, pretty much everybody in my class
at school was related in one way or another, but Jenny and I
were related on the Haala side. Her dad and my mom were
cousins.

It's called gay, she said. Liking other men is called being
gay. Like my dad's brother and his uncle. Everybody knows
about the gays, but no one talks about it. Because it's a sin,
you know. Sex is for making babies only, and two men can't
make a baby when they have sex, so you can go to Hell for it.

Well, I said, why would two men want a baby anyway?

You don't get it. God, how can you be so dumb?

Mom knew Milly carried a litter when she started nipping at the corn stalks sprouting tall in the garden and dancing accordion-like in the noon of the day. Dogs do crazy things when they're gettin' a litter, she said. A couple of months later, Milly's underbody bulged like a bread loaf. Indecent, said Mom when Milly licked her milk heavy teats. Mom kicked Milly's belly.

One day the dog sauntered head low, tail dipped, into the machine shed, so Annie Jo and I followed and from the fender of the John Deere 4010 watched her expel thirteen puppies and gulp the afterbirth. In the shadow of our combine's tire, where Annie Jo had laid an old blanket, Milly lapped clean their noses, between their hinds, and around their ears, swabbing white matter off, her tongue dabbing all their pleats the way Mom ironed all the folds of my St. Mary's school uniform to keep Sister Gertrude from aiming at me with the long end of her cross and saying, What would Jesus say about such carelessness with your clothing? He'd strip you bare and give your uniform to the Africans, who would know how to appreciate it. The puppies clambered over Milly like ants in butter. Annie Jo sat there all afternoon even after I got bored and went to help Dad feed the calves. Mom came to get her for supper, and they walked back to the house. Mom's building belly busted the air before them, and

Annie Jo's long hair, whipped by the wind, trailed after. Together they looked a slowly comet.

Milly's litter grew into long-haired, long-nosed lab-shepherd crosses in a puzzle of colors patched together. They streaked across the yard, and Mom said, God, those are ugly animals. And not a stitch of sense. Dad put an ad in the *Sleepy Eye Herald Dispatch* under "Giveaway." Thirteen healthy lab/shepherd cross puppies. Free. Call 506–793–7808, it read.

Annie Jo and I prayed for each puppy by name in a decade of the rosary every night before bed, even though it was summer and I didn't have to keep up on my prayer chart for school. We said extra Hail Marys to make sure each dog had its own special intention. An Our Father for Milly, thirteen Hail Marys for her pups, and a Glory Be for our coming baby.

Summers brought the heat and dirt I liked, but I always missed Jenny. All summer, I stocked up stories to tell her, to write her. When school started again, instead of comparing new shoes, barrettes, or erasers, we created homemade cartoons. Hers started like this:

A boxed picture of two figures dressed in biblical garb, labeled Virgin Mary and St. Peter. The caption read, *Hey Virgin Mary, how do you like my staff?* She dropped it on my desk on her way to the pencil sharpener.

I drew an adjacent box, the same two characters, wrote, *Well Peter, it's the nicest staff I've ever seen*, slid the note back with the sole of my shoe.

It's so heavy, will you hold it for me?

And the cartoons always ended the same—two biblical characters rolling around on the ground, kicking up dust. I folded the paper, stuck it in my shoe, and hid it at home to enjoy in the summer. She did the same, only her mom was more curious than mine, and found a bunch of stories Jenny wrote about the school counselor, which she turned in to the principal. Jenny had meetings with Father John for several weeks. We didn't write so much after that.

Mom's belly swelled seven times. She got one dead baby and six daughters out of the process: Dad's boy, me, Annie Jo, Natty, Lila, Dakota, and Mia. We came around every three years or so, like grasshopper cycles. There's poison left in our women after a birth. It circles and spits and fights against our sinew and matter and rides our synapses, stings our nerves, and lingers long. Mom's face sagged with desolation. Her eyes dissolved into her cheeks. Her cheeks into her chin, her chin to her neck, and her body went on that way to her toes. Her curves and softness that used to make the men look twice only appeared once in a while after Lila, the fourth, was born. Then Dakota came, and about a year later, Mia. After her, the doctors sterilized Mom because her body had tried to abort Mia. Mom's blood attacked the baby's, and as soon as Mia was viable, the doctors induced labor. The tiny creature, jaundiced and small as God would allow a living child, could hardly cry, and Mom was thankful for that. Already at home were a husband—drunk mostly, gambling away the farm and running around—a high school junior with a walk too grown-up and a mind too distrusting of the school and church for her own good, an eighth grader wearing an angst wrinkle in her forehead already and a smart mouth besides, a sixth grader—the one who looked just like him—sitting at the window, scratching the varnish off the wood frame, waiting for her dad to come home and making up excuses for him when he didn't, a third grader burdened with picking up the little ones' toys, bottles, and diapers without enough time for play, and a toddler still in diapers asking, pulling, grabbing, and yanking things from Mom at every waking moment. She'd say and say and say, Why can't you just leave me be? Get off me. Leave me be. You're all choking me. She scratched at her neck and ran her fingers up and down her arms. She closed herself in her room with Mia for privacy and cried several months straight. Dakota, just one year, Lila, and Natty became the charge of Annie Jo and me when we weren't in school and Grandma when we were. Mom didn't wake us for school, didn't come to games, didn't check homework. She didn't eat. She couldn't sleep at night. And the only sounds that came from the room were moans and sobs and Mia's kitten cries. Sometimes Mom came out to warm a bottle, and then she lifted her lip and screamed at me or Annie Jo or Natty for a half hour, then stole into a lifeless silence for days. Grandma said, It's just a little case of the baby blues and she'll snap out of it.

I worked at Subway in Sleepy Eye with Jenny in high school, after Mom had my fourth and fifth sisters. I told

Jenny about Mom on our common shifts, between slicing tomatoes and onions and peppers and sending away all the girlfriends of Jenny's high school lovers. Jenny said Mom had Post-Partum Depression and she needed medication, but she'd be alright. And, Colie, I'm leaving early. If Anthony comes in while I'm out, tell him I need money for birth control and he's paying this time. Do you want me to make an appointment for you? You really should be on it. You could hide pills easy enough from your mom.

No, I said. I'm fine. I'll tell him if he comes in.

One night, when I came home from my weekend late shift, I found Mom, head back and eyes closed, in the rocking chair, holding a bottle in Mia's mouth. The milk spilled down the side of the baby's mouth and dampened her sleeper. I pulled the bottle from Mom's hand, shook and roused her.

Mom, I said, you're spilling. I'll feed Mia and put her to bed.

Oh God, she said, I fell asleep. You smell like smoke. Have you been smoking? You're allergic, you know.

No, Mom. Scott smokes. It's from him.

I don't like you slutting around with him. I've heard about him. Don't you dare come home pregnant. Don't you dare or you'll be out of this house and I mean it.

Mom. Don't talk so dirty.

You'll never have a shittin' moment's peace if you do.

Go to bed, Mom.

I'm going. Thank you, Nicole. Good night.

Before she could get up the stairs, Dakota cried out, too,

and Mom went to the nursery, picked up Dakota, and stepped back down the stairs to warm another bottle. She settled into the other chair, and we sat in the dark together feeding the babies, rocking our way into the early morning blue.

A few months later, when Dad left her for a bank teller over in Rochester, she said good riddance. And a relaxed forehead came to her when we girls found ourselves husbands. I got mine at nineteen. Annie Jo hers at twenty-one, and Natty moved to Rochester with Dad when she was eighteen and that was all the same to Mom. She was counting down the tasks.

The first hint of a baby in your nineteen-year-old belly comes as a memory of yourself as a girl hiding behind the house, picking soft clumps of soil from beneath the patch of lilies of the valley and placing them on your tongue, sucking the water and mineral and blood from the dirt. Girls will try to suck life from anything. This baby, this daughter, in your stomach requires more energy than you have, and so the cravings for the earth on your tongue begin again. On your wedding day, you pull leaves and petals from the bouquets and pop them in your mouth. You feel your daughter's quickening in your womb, calling for more green, dirt, earth, energy, life, all down the aisle. Your dad's not there—he's off with his bank teller, you suppose, so your mom grips your right elbow and your little sister Dakota holds your left hand all the way to the groom waiting at the altar. Jenny leads the bridesmaids. She's a mother already herself. And this is the beginning of the time, the years, in which you will not rely on her anymore. You've learned this from your mother. Don't complain. Don't burden friends. And when Jenny calls your home in the months to come and says, Nicole, you're getting all sucked up in his life, what about yours?, you'll pass her off as selfish and she'll stop calling. Mia, just two years old, follows behind, clomps on your train then and again. The Haalas and Helgets and relatives of your fiancé laugh at their antics, smile at their billowy dresses. You hear, *Oh, what will those little ones do without their Colie around all the time?* You wonder too.

Seven months after your wedding day, the doctors induce labor and pry a daughter, red and angry and bald, from you, and ten weeks later you conceive a son. Through nausea and exhaustion, you dance and walk the daughter, colic-ridden, around the kitchen floor while a ball of another baby forms beneath her bottom. Your stomach becomes a support of sorts for your daughter, your breasts, pillows. The first you see of your boy is a stream of urine arcing over the delivery room doctor and onto the floor. *Well I guess we know what he thinks of this world,* your doctor jokes. But you know the baby boy's serious. He weighs eight and a half pounds, is twenty-four inches long. His jaw is crooked because he's been pressed against your hip, and your pelvis will never be right again. You gained fifteen pounds during your pregnancy. You weigh less than before you were pregnant by the time you leave the hospital thirty-six hours later. *Oh, you're so lucky,* the nurses say. *You'll be in your jeans the minute you get home.* You don't tell them that between bouncing and carrying your daughter and being sick with this baby, you couldn't eat a thing and the baby's suffered for it. The pediatrician says he's iron deficient and jaundiced already. You and the baby are put on an iron supplement. Your husband has to work, so he can't bring you and baby home from the hospital. Your mom says she can't pick you up, but she's sure you'll think of something. Finally, your grandma comes to get you. But before you can go home, she needs to *stop quick at Cub Foods to pick up a couple of things. It'll only take a few minutes. All right then?* And it's while wandering through that grocery store with a newborn in your arms and a baby in the cart and post-natal blood soaking the pad the nurses gave you, you feel your mom's legacy settle in your mind. You look at all the food and want to throw up. You smell your own blood and want to throw up. You see white uterine mucus behind the baby's ear, in the folds of his neck, and want to throw up. You buy a package of newborn diapers, a package of size threes. You buy extra large Kotex for yourself. The blood will keep coming for six weeks.

At home, alone with these babies, a turning and yearning twists on some days and moves you frantic, and on others, only your babies' needs can coax you out of bed—that and the possibility someone might stop by unannounced. You look at those babies and wonder how such things became entrusted to you. The incessant crying drives you to pace up and down with them on your shoulder all afternoon, and a voice that isn't yours, but maybe an older, wiser version of you, tells you that these babies hate you and that you are terrible at this job. You cry over the guilt of them both crying. You eat only grapes and Jolly Ranchers. You drink Dr. Pepper and coffee. You can't sleep, but you can't stay awake. You walk babies constantly. You put your hand on the phone at least once a month and consider calling Jenny, but never do. A perpetual drool mark spots your shoulder. You wear clothes stained with spit-up, underwear with blood. A constant ache strains your right arm. Your hair falls out in clumps from hormonal changes. You have lumps the size of eyeballs in your armpits from infected mammary glands, but, sometimes, you hope it's cancer. You hope the cancer spreads its wicked strands up into your brain and stops the loneliness and living. And you put the babies side by side and thank God for them. You wonder at their perfect noses, fingernails, and eyelashes, and you love them. You love them so hard, you don't deserve them. And the voice agrees, the voice tells you to quit this pretense, to do these children a favor and drop yourself down the stairs and break your neck or sit in the bathtub and butcher-knife the whites of your wrists. Do it right before you expect your husband home so that the children aren't left alone for long. But you never know exactly when he'll be home.

They'll be fine, the voice says. Don't be paranoid.

You tell the voice to quiet. And you determine to show everybody that you are so used to this, so good at this that you refuse to let anyone else hold your babies, cuddle them, soothe them. You do everything yourself. And when you get the babies to sleep at night, and then shower and go to bed yourself, your husband's there, waiting. And for a while, you are a willing wife, but it doesn't take long before you loathe his heat, his heartbeat, his breath. You sleep on the couch.

Annie Jo got a boy nine months after her wedding day, and a girl came just a bit later. Dad wasn't watching too close, so Natty took in a drug dealer and she had his son before she was twenty. The babies keep coming in this family, and while we love our babies, we detest ourselves and wrestle against anything and everything to deny and prove it. We live paradox. We're restless; we fixate with thoughts about our sagging breasts and lopsided hips and falling-out hair and the dark rings under our eyes and we wonder about who our working husbands are talking to and thirty-days-late bills and lispy sons who pronounce *lion* like *wion* and daughters who won't make friends and hide behind our legs because we've coddled them too long and our toddlers who bite, hit, clobber other kids with plastic bats or tree branches and we wonder what will ever become of us when all these kids have gone. We think about how we burned the bread and dried out the chicken and how our mother lifts the lid of our supper pot and says, *Well, this looks different. New recipe?*

Our bodies don't relax. We can't sit still. We bake and cook, though no one's hungry, to mess dishes so we can wash and dry them seven or eight times a day. We iron bed sheets, boxers, and t-shirts. Spend hours trying to pair white socks. Repaint the walls every time a little one leaves a smudge.

Change the kids' clothes in the morning, afternoon, and evening and throw all clothes, hardly worn, into the laundry basket. We check on our infants every thirty minutes all dark night to make sure they're breathing, put our hands on their backs to feel the rise and fall, and, just to be certain, we poke them until they stir and wake for another round of feeding, changing, or rocking back to sleep. We keep the laundry coming, the washing machine spinning, dryer humming, and iron sizzling all day long. We lug the clothes baskets up and down the stairs, spill socks over the side, bump our elbows against door frames. Move all the furniture and steam clean the carpets each month. And when we're bored, we'll create a conflict, instigate a battle, or slip quietly into our minds and think and speak to no one for days, put tension in the air. We do all these ordinary things and think all these ordinary thoughts, but we can't reconcile them normally. We like to fight. And, as our dad always used to say, we've got our ma in us, alright. We have a way of making a man love us and suffer him for doing it. Smart as whips, people always said of us. And those genes. Those Helget girls are something else. Yep, Dad said. My girls are beauties, alright. God help any man who takes them on, though.

Milly's thirteen puppies grew up, round, wild, and rambunctious. They tousled under Mom's Big Boy tomato plants, chased leaping grasshoppers, and knocked the plump fruit to the ground, sniffed and bit them, ruined them with their play. I watched from the kitchen window. Mom, wearing

Dad's т-shirt, shooed them out of her vegetable garden with a broom. Get out of here, you little bastards, she yelled. Mom could swear like a man. Each time she raised the broom, her tummy showed between her lifted shirt and pants, her belly button protruded because, she told Annie Jo and me, the baby kicked it out. Annie Jo ran round trying to chase the pack out of the garden, her hair flying behind her with words to Mom, too. Mom. Stop. You're going to hurt them. You're going to hurt the baby, she said. Mom didn't stop swinging, but she did cup one arm under the swell of her stomach, braced it as she wielded the broom one-handed, down and down again. Grasshoppers flashed around her like hot grease. I grabbed a package of bologna from the refrigerator and headed outside. Annie Jo ran to me from the garden and took a few slices. We teased the puppies with the meat to tempt them out. They came. Mom bent over her stomach to salvage some of the tomatoes. Begging, the puppies pounced and wound around my legs. One jumped up on my thigh and scratched a mark. Two bounced in front of me, and I tripped. When I hit the ground, my elbow bit gravel. Damn bastards, I muttered. Annie Jo shushed me and helped me up by the arm. She picked stuck gravel out of my bleeding with her fingernails, and the puppies grabbed the dropped package of bologna and tore away, fighting and growling.

Mom could cook. And she could garden, can fruits and vegetables, bake, and make our hundred-year-old farmhouse warm and comfortable. The supper table bulged with enormous beef or pork roasts, mashed, fried, or boiled potatoes, pan gravy, creamed or baked vegetables, stewed or jellied fruits, or homemade bread most nights when we girls were young, while Dad was at home with us and between Mom's gloomy times. If we cleared our plates, Mom tipped them over to the clean side and planted a slice of pie or cake or a bar on there. This system kept us from asking for dessert without finishing our supper. We circled our arms around our plates and hovered above them, protecting our food like skinny, jealous cats. The babies and even Dad couldn't be stopped from stabbing forks at chunks of meat or sliding their spoons into somebody else's pie.

Dad's brothers hopped out of their chairs for Mom's stuffing at holiday gatherings. She spent days cooking meat and saving the broth, deboning and pushing chicken through a hand-crank grinder, cubing and drying potato bread, slicing celery and onion, and baking a supply large enough to feed all fifty-some relatives on Dad's side. Uncle Tweet and Uncle Tubby would sneak up behind her when she carried that economy-size roaster into Grandma Helget's house, lift the lid, and pinch the crusty edges off the top and pop it into their mouths. Not even Grandma could perfect Mom's stuffing.

Get out of there now, she'd say. Worse than kids, you are. But she was teasing; she liked Dad's brothers, and they liked her pretty face and sassy charm. She was good enough to keep her shadows from them and her sisters-in-law, too. And if she couldn't trust herself to be good, she made up an excuse and stayed home.

Mom's creative mind went to work on her garden and in her meals and in food preservation. Clear jars with gold rims for our garden tomatoes, crushed and whole, lined full rows in the basement canning room. Purple beets lay sliced and stacked in wine-colored juice. Two rows of pickled cucumbers stood straight in brine just right. Mom chose the most uniform jars and sent me off to the county fair with them. She stood a few feet from the judge and listened to me talk about choosing the best sized and best textured and best flavored cucumbers from the vine, scrubbing them with a wash cloth so as not to scratch the skin, picking the freshest dill, trapping the seasonings in a cheese cloth or baby sock, and boiling those jars to seal them properly, to prevent botulism. I earned Grand Champion and was sent to the state fair. The state fair judges slapped a purple ribbon on my jars, too, and the newspaper snapped my picture, which Mom cut out and taped to the refrigerator.

And Mom always had her fingers in her girls' hair. Braiding, twisting, brushing, washing, and binding. The curling iron lay hot all Sunday morning until Mass. One after another, we girls took our turns sitting on the counter or the toilet seat and letting Mom twist the bands and steam the curls into place. Mom's hands fluttered and wrung all round the house. Her sensibilities went wild at times, like when she planted a whole new grove of trees in one week and tended to the watering and pruning for the next few weeks until the roots took and the trees could tend to themselves, or when she called Mathiowetz Construction to come bulldoze and bury all the outbuildings—granaries, pig barns, chicken coops, and bins. But trees, shrubs, flowers, and vegetables spread and greened up under her hand. Her mind intuited complimentary colors and shapes. Blue flowers behind yellow. Purple against orange. Blooming shrubs, tall, next to squat cedars. Spreads of lily of the valley under the shade of the big cottonwood tree. She had never been formally trained in horticulture or cooking or hairdressing. She just knew. She knew how to put things together, and these things became her art and her hand and mind-busying outlet.

Let's say no one ever shows you a painting by Picasso or Van Gogh or Monet or Frida. Say you've seen no nude forms with green, red, and blue facial features, no vases of sunflowers with paint strokes the size of thick jerky, no dizzying splatters of color that somehow create a poppy field and a strolling woman, no masculine women with hair on their lips, their brows. Let's say the only art you see is the stained glass windows of reverent martyrs, women who died rather than sacrifice their chastity and men who converted others to Catholicism by the blade of a sword, and statues of a benevolent Virgin bowing before her son and her husband and her God. What will you learn of the world, of its order, of your role in it? If your school can't afford an art teacher or art class and doodling is behavior worthy of detention, when will you pick up a pencil for drawing? Can you learn about wifehood and motherhood and womanhood from the books the superintendent of the school, a priest, chooses for you?

What happens to children and teenagers when
prominent literary reference in any class is the Bibl
you read over and over that women are tricksters l   ..,
bitter, jealous wives like Sarah, seducers like Esther, what
happens to your perspective, your perception? What if
you must spend enormous amounts of time memorizing
prayers—the Act of Contrition, the Apostles' Creed, the Acts
of Faith, Hope, and Love, the decades of the rosary, the Holy
Days of Obligation, the Seven Gifts of the Holy Spirit, the
Seven Deadly Sins—and what if as soon as you memorize
those, there are new prayers to memorize? What if you re-
peat ideas instead of questioning theories and philosophy
and tradition? What if you do this until you can't think on
your own? But what if, maybe, you still have an ounce of creativity in you and you write little stories in your notebooks
and they're good, decent anyway, and you make your friend
Jenny laugh when she reads them and she responds with
funnier, racier, sexier stories, but she gets caught and the
tolerance for writing creatively becomes zero in your school
and certainly at home where writing is considered idleness?
What if, instead of discovering the Truth, you are told the
Truth, and are told any variance from it will result in Hell?
What if you grow up believing this, and you have children?
What if you teach them the same things?

In a black mid-week night of Annie Jo's fifth month of pregnancy, her husband rang our phone, asked if I could come get
Annie Jo out of the bathroom.

She locked herself in there and is raising hell, he said. I can't take it. I'm not used to this.

She's fine, I said.

What's wrong with her? Should I call the hospital? Holy shit, man, she wasn't like this before, was she? I've never seen any blasted thing like it. It can't be normal.

Call Mom, I told him.

Colie. Don't hang up. Please. I did that already and she said to call you. She said *Leave me be and don't call here again with Annie Jo's nonsense.*

I was pregnant myself. I told him to ignore Annie Jo, don't pay any attention to her, that she'd be fine. Don't worry. She just gets a little wild sometimes and who wouldn't? She's just fuming. Let her get it out of her system for a while. You two'll laugh about it tomorrow.

I doubt it, Colie. I can't take this type of thing. She says she's gonna rip the baby from her body.

Oh, sometimes I feel like ripping this baby from my belly, too. Can't hardly stand it. Big as a whale.

But she's screaming it. She *means* it.

Yeah. I can hear her through the phone. Just tell her the neighbors'll hear. That should settle her down a bit. Tell her the neighbors'll hear and probably call the cops and she wouldn't want that, now would she?

Eight weeks and no one had called about a pup.

Mom spoke to Dad that evening. I watched a M*A*S*H rerun on the kitchen TV and washed bruised and bursting tomatoes at the counter. I imagined myself blond and beautiful as Hot Lips as I wiped them clean and cut out the stems, hummed the opening theme, and passed the dirtless and destemmed tomatoes to Mom for juicing. She crushed the red, watery fruit into a thin secretion while Dad sat at the kitchen table eating ham chops and fried potatoes. Annie Jo buttered several slices of rye bread for him and piled them on a plate, kept buttering and stacking because he could eat a whole loaf in a sitting. On the counter, jars sparkled waiting for the tomato juice. Huge kettles of water boiled on the gas stove. The steam from the boil and the heat from the summer stewed the kitchen air.

Mom interrupted Dad's dinner, said to him, You've got to get rid of them. They're eating us out of house and home.

Dad kept chewing.

They've wrecked most of my vegetables, and they dig huge holes in my flower beds. Dump them in the river. It'll be an easy way. Clean, too. If I have to kick one more damn dog out of my way, I'm going to slice the entire litter with a paring knife and boil them for supper.

Dad put down his fork. How's a man supposed to eat around here, he wanted to know.

I looked at Annie Jo. She stopped buttering bread, chewed her lip, and scraped in her hair with the butter knife where I had pulled a tick off her earlier.

Oh, I'm just kidding. Don't get all weepy now, she said to Annie Jo. I'm just teasing. Mom started laughing so that tears came and she wet her pants.

Oh shit, she said. I've got to pee every five minutes with this baby pushing on my bladder. She grabbed a dish towel and cupped it between her legs, wobbled to the bathroom. When she came out, she reminded Dad to bag and toss them over the Little Cottonwood Bridge. Drown them.

Woman, watch it, Dad said. You're wild again.

When he was a kid swimming with his brothers, Dad almost drowned in the Little Cottonwood River. Uncle Sue saved his life with a tree branch. He was afraid of water since and wouldn't go near it. He wouldn't drown them. He pushed his plate away and lifted his shirt to wipe his face clean.

Shoot 'em, then, Mom said, or I will. You've got to accept that nobody's gonna call. They're mutts.

The T-shirt clung to her. Damp stains spread over her breasts and under her arms, a mixture of readying milk and wet salt. Her jutting nipples and belly button added topography to the baby mound.

God, this kid won't rest. She'll be a nervous one, I can tell. It's another girl. You won't get your boy, yet, William. Not yet. And this one's going to be called Natalie. Isn't that pretty?

Mom opened the cupboard door and grabbed the Tylenol. Tapped three or four into her palm and swallowed them one at a time dry. She turned to Dad who was still sitting at the table.

So, she said, are you gonna shoot them shittin' dogs or what?

I glanced at the wound on my elbow. The outer edges were beginning to scab. Inside it looked like tomatoes, red and watery.

. . .

Mom found cigarettes in Natty's pocket in sixth grade, beer under her bed in seventh, marijuana on her dresser in eighth. By the end of the next year, Natty's eyes ran nervous with red veins, caused by crank, mushrooms, cocaine, and ecstasy. Natty gave up most as soon as she discovered she was pregnant, just smoked pot once in a while.

It's less harmful than cigarettes, you know, she said. Practically harmless. And it sure helps calm my nerves, and it can't be good for the baby anyway if I'm at my wit's end all the time.

No, we said. That can't be good.

But after her son turned one, when she started in on crank and mushrooms again and her boyfriend started dealing from Dad's home, social services took the baby, who was just starting to walk, away from her. Because Preston's dad was in jail and didn't have any parental rights, Mom had legal custody of Preston should Natty become incapacitated. But Mom said to let him go up for adoption, she had her own kids to raise and couldn't be expected to have another child underfoot all the livelong day.

Annie Jo and I said we'd take the baby. He's our own blood, for crying out loud, and what would people think? Sending our own family off to adoption after an entire year's passed never to be seen again? Who does a thing like that?

I guess, Mom said. Yes. That's true. What would people think?

Mom swept down to social services and picked the baby up and moved him in with her, Lila, Dakota, and Mia. She put Dakota and Mia in charge of him. When Natty finished up her treatment, Mom moved her in, too. Mom dressed the entire crew up for Mass every Sunday and returned Father John's supportive grin with an *Oh, isn't this what any good mother would do?* look. Natty picked scabs or wiped the baby's nose with her sleeve over and over until the tiny thing bled during Mass, and Mom finally stopped making her go because she was too much of a nervous wreck, caused too much commotion, squirreled around like a caged animal, and Mom thought everybody was whispering *withdrawal*.

A few days after that dinner, Dad locked Milly in the granary. Mom told me to get a package of bologna, lead those pups into the milkroom, and close the door behind me. Annie Jo, you stay up by the house. Annie Jo went to the counter and picked a tomato. Her eyes followed me to the refrigerator. I didn't look, but I felt them.

The puppies chased me into the confines of the milkroom. As soon as all thirteen were in, Mom said, Stay put now, and she shut the steel door, leaving us in the bowel of the barn. I opened the package of bologna and gave a slice to each pup. They greedily ate and tried to steal from each other. I held back one bologna slice. They frolicked under the bulk tank that held the milk and behind the refrigerator that held Dad's Hauenstein beer and various bottles of animal medicines and antibiotics. I overturned a pail, sat, and watched them play. The thirteen of them reminded me of Annie Jo's favorite candy, jelly beans. They looked like a loosened handful of them, roly and round in their playfulness, speckled and mismatched. I balled the last slice of bologna in my palm. I was glad Dad was to shoot them. I didn't want them to bear Mom's paring knife.

A puppy lifted its leg and peed on the support of the steel sink. A yellow pool worked its way into a stream on the cemented floor, followed the incline that led it to the drain in the center of the room. The cool of the floor felt fine under my feet while I considered this. They jumped about on their paws, and I wondered if they could appreciate the chill of the floor.

The white walls of the milkroom looked a little like the gynecologist's office Mom visited. Both smelled of sanitizer. I supposed that the nurses in the gynecologist's office couldn't hose down the floor and walls of the office, though. That's what we did. We hosed them down in the milkroom and the dirty water flowed straight into the drain, leaving clean walls and a clean floor behind. I always went with her to these appointments. She was going once a week by then. The doctor worried about Mom's condition because of the other baby who lay in limbo, according to Sister Gertrude. The doctor let me hear the baby's heartbeat through his stethoscope sometimes. He put on rubber gloves and reached deep inside her to determine, as Mom explained, when the baby was coming. It made a sound like crushing tomatoes when he removed his fingers from her. And when the doctor asked Mom how she was feeling, *really,* Mom looked him straight in the face and said, Oh just fine, thank you very much. I feel so healthy when I'm pregnant. Never better. We're made for having babies on my side. We've got the hips for it alright.

Nobody mentions it—the way you look, smell, scream, or don't talk. When you open the door, baby bundled in one arm, and sisters, aunts, Mom, and Grandma step through the door, your eyes can be red and puffy as raw chicken and wet from tears that've welled and poured all day or black and swollen from sleeplessness or jittery and lashless from relentless rubbing and scratching. They'll set down wrapped presents, glance at you quick, look away, then peel back the blanket from the baby, and say, My, aren't you proud? What a head of hair. Looks like a content one, too. God, you're lucky. Mine cried day and night for hours and hours. I never got a moment's rest. Colic and indigestion and reflux and diaper rash, too. Spitting up constantly. And, boy, you've dropped that baby weight quick. Good Lord, you must be down to a hundred pounds. Oh, these girls and their small frames. They get that from the Helget side, you know. Our side's thick. We Haala women have boobs, hips, butts full and thick as good steaks. Curves everywhere. You girls—all bone and angles. You're lucky to get that from your dad. He wasn't worth much, but at least he was slim. But you should eat. I brought a hotdish. Do you want me to throw it in? The hubby must be getting hungry. Keep him fed or you'll have another baby on your hands. Those men. They're worse than kids.

Yes, you think. Worse than kids. And though you smile and wish your husband a good day when he leaves for work at the co-op, you pray that this'll be the last time you see him. You watch his tail lights drive off and put your hand against the cool window and think, Wouldn't it be nice if this were the last image of him, two red bulbs shrinking away? You blame him. You think he's trapped you. You hope he'll find another woman who can stand his hand on the small of her back that means he's ready for the third time that week. You hate the way he presses himself against you and rolls you over. He unfolds you like a game board. Hands, arms, legs. You stare at the wall or the ceiling and the window and wonder who invented this behavior, this process. You detest his primacy. You detest his body. You detest yours. When he's finished, you lock yourself in the bathroom, turn the shower to the hottest setting your skin can stand. You rub your fingers over the stretch marks on your breasts and hips and stomach. You think maybe he could get a girlfriend who doesn't need sex therapy and who wears the matching bra and panty sets he buys and who watches the Oprah shows he's taped for you where she interviews depressed housewives who avoid sex. And while Oprah doesn't help your sex drive or body image, she does introduce *She's Come Undone* and then *A Map of the World* and then *The Poisonwood Bible* and *Where the Heart Is* and *White Oleander*, and you plant one baby on the floor with the toys and the other in your arms with the bottle and you read. You won't lift your eyes when your husband opens the door home and hungry from work.

Could you put that book down for two seconds and give me the time of day? he says. And that baby's six months old and doesn't need to be held all the time and definitely doesn't need to be in our bed any longer. Are you listening to me? Can you talk? Are you mute all of a sudden? Talk to me for God's sakes. I'm so sick of this passive aggressive shit. It's old.

You hope maybe he'll grow lonely and leave, or get too tired from the crying babies and fly away, or crash his car on the commute, or die a quick heart-attack death from all the red meat you feed him. You encourage him to go deer hunting with his friend Brent, who is careless, hopeless, and brainless with a rifle, swinging the loaded thing left and right as if he were wrestling a wild snake. You smile at the way he mixes fertilizer, herbicide, and insecticide with his bare hands. You laugh when a hose of anhydrous ammonia, fertilizer that'll melt the eyes right out of a person's skull, explodes on him and he's caught in a cloud of the burning gas and has to hold his breath and run from there eyes closed. You imagine brain aneurisms. You imagine cancer cells winding up his testicles into his body and poisoning him. At the very least, you think, couldn't he just get laryngitis for a while? You trace his family medical history looking for any genetic flaw. Lots of heart problems. Diabetes, too. That's good. You're sure all your problems would be solved if he were gone.

But then you feel guilty. You ask God what is wrong with you. He's a good man, loves you, loves his kids. He deserves better than you. What could this man have possibly done to warrant you wishing his death?

So you wish for yours. But you know the babies need their

mother. And the guilt of such a thing would kill you for sure; it's the sort of guilt that transcends death.

Dad opened the steel door and put himself between it and the frame to prevent the puppies from escaping. A stream of natural light and heat invaded the winter neatness of the milkroom. He carried his .410 under his arm and a package of shells in his hand. The puppies exploded into excited familiarity. When he milked cows, Dad always gave them the sopping milk filters to chew and poured the last few sips of his Hauenstein into their water bowls.

Okay, he said, out with you. Put the pail away before you go.

I put the pail away. The puppies scampered after me on my way to the door. Dad warned me against loosening them out. His voice was low and tired. I threw the ball of bologna into the opposite corner of the milkroom. The puppies raced for it, and I slipped out the door and onto the heated gravel. As I turned to close the door, I caught Dad's face: a pile of misery, dark circles cupped his eyes, his lips faded thin.

Well, he said, maybe them being gone will please your ma for a while, huh?

He looked at me. I turned away and closed the door behind me.

I glanced across the yard. Mom tapped watermelons with her fist in the garden. On the stump of a cottonwood tree, leaves, branches, trunk brought down by disease before we were born, Annie Jo sat eating another tomato. Next to her, a ham bone from last night's dinner lay, a consolation gift for Milly once we let her out.

I leaned against the wall of the milkroom for a second. Briefly, I imagined wild pellets from the shells penetrating the wall and invading my back, but I knew it was impossible. Not enough force from a .410. I sank to the ground and listened for the shots.

You can't do your mom's life. You're lonely, you're sad. You have pent-up yearnings and old despondency that can't be reconciled in this marriage, with this man, in this house, in this town, in this life. You meet someone else. It's almost cliché, you know, wanting someone else just seven years into a marriage. But, at twenty-seven, you quit your marriage, explain to your kids about divorce and tell them that families take all shapes and move them to another town and another life. Your mother stops speaking to you because you are not hiding problems from everyone else, the way she's always managed. You try to talk to her; you sob, tell her about the melancholy that's hung around your feet since you were little and the despair that's come to you in your twenties. You tell her secrets you've never told anyone else before. She's quiet for a moment, then says, that's life. This is life. It's miserable. She uses the secrets you told her to convince the rest of your family you're crazy and not to be believed or trusted or spoken to. Your mom and Annie Jo side with your ex-husband, encourage him to try to take the children away from you. Your little sisters follow course.

Except Natty, who's cleaned up, raises her son on her own, and doesn't care what your Mom says about the sin and shame of anything. Your mom refuses to accept your decision, says it's selfish and that you should think about what's best for your kids.

You know this move is selfish, but maintain that you need it, that your kids will benefit from it, too.

Screw her, Natty says of your mom. She's about as nuts as they get.

Your dad calls. He offers his help, wants to meet his grandkids, wants to see you.

Sure, you tell him, but first you should know, I've met someone else.

Well, I know a little something about that, I guess. Think through it, Colie. Be sure it's right for you and for your kids.

I have, Dad. I have already.

This other man says you're creative, articulate, and beautiful. Funny, too.

Ha, you laugh. Seriously? you say.

He listens to your stories about growing up. You tell him about your grandma, a little girl buried alive, your dad's baseball bat, your mom's girls, your crazy uncle, the notes and cartoons you and Jenny used to write, your church and the priest. He tells you to write these stories down, tells you to call Jenny. So you do. You talk about dreams you have for your kids and things you'd like to see and places you'd like to go. You look at a map together, tap Lake Victoria, Rio, Paris.

I'll take you, he says. I'll hide you in my back pocket. I'll be good to you. I'll be good to the kids.

The voice comes back to warn you not to encourage his attention. Do everybody a favor and step away from this. Keep your lunacy to yourself.

But he kisses you. He undresses you. His weight on top of your body that has satisfied a seven-year husband, birthed three children, is toughened from their pawing, their pulling, their dangling legs, is numb with housecleaning and laundry and pretending, keeps you from fighting against yourself finally. You feel a passion, a natural, healthy passion that you have never felt before. He holds the long lean of himself against your skin and bone and stays steady so you can feel his pulse. You move against him, and he says to wait, be still. He's close and heavy on your belly, your chest. He traces your stretch marks, bites your hips, kisses your stomach. And when you are rested and patient, he rocks and pushes. He presses down, and you close your eyes and fall into the blankets. The gust of your life blows against your back, rolls over your sides, lifts your fingers, your hair, tempts you to ride with it, but you don't. You let it go. Memories—your mom's swollen belly, her red eyes, your dad's brandy breath, his strong hands, your sisters' waning cries, Grandma's stories, stretched faces and hurried sounds—speed past you and up and beyond your reach, but still visible. And maybe your legacy will be nothing more than the tremors you leave on these sheets, this bed, floor, the gravel, and the very plates of this soil or the stains you leave on the elements—marrow and muscle you've planted in the earth, blood you've rinsed with water, secrets the wind blows to your children, and embers you've left glowing in their bodies: intensity, desperation, and wildness. You sink below the earth and ash and coffins of dead relatives and sandy river beds and memories and animal bones and cottonwood roots and blood stains generations deep and insects and your voices and demons in the core blazing with shame and regrets and hate and suspicion and you try to leave them there. And, for a while, he doesn't let you up. He cuts your breaths to a few long whispers until you're so tired and so subdued and so low, you can only come up.

But this is only a start to the work you need to do. You can't be kissed awake like the princesses of Isabella's fairy tale books. You've got to fix your mind and your body yourself. Your dad and mom, above all else, built you to manage things, to mend from the outside in. And there's a truth in this lesson. Heal the body and the mind does follow. The Minnesota winter still rolls you over and drops its gray on your chest. You're still difficult on those short dark days. You still get quiet. You still get angry. You still like to fight. You still trouble yourself with ordinary things. And your wildness raises his eyebrows, and your silence makes him yell, makes him hold his head in his hands and cry. He says, Nicole, you have a demon inside you. We've got to do something about it. And this time, you agree. You speak about the devils that haunt you, about the old habits you hold. And when you can see them and name them, you can begin casting them out and throwing them down.

· · ·

After, Mom and I carried the weight of the bodies from the milkroom to the manure spreader. Annie Jo watched from the stump through teary crevices of fingers. One large maroon hole surrounded by flecks of smaller ones gaped in the bodies of Milly's pups scattered in a constellation over the floor. In each one erupted a galaxy of planets and stars created by pellets that separated from the cluster. Before I picked up the first pup, I ran my fingers over the hollows the pellets left in its skin, and the body felt living still and wet with red spreading over, thick and sticky in its fur. I carried them one at a time, entire body, across my arms. I cradled them. Mom grabbed puppies two at a time, snatched them by a tail, a paw, an ear even, swinging bodies like groceries to the spreader. We threw them in with the cow mess, and they landed with a suck. When the last one was in, Mom said, Boy, am I glad to be done with that, and she looked like a peace had settled on her. Dad spread the puppies' bodies with the manure out in the back forty later for fertilizer. Mom hosed down the walls and floor of the milkroom until the water running to the drain lost its pink tint. Annie Jo walked ham bone in hand to the granary. Her little bare feet spread grass, nervous with grasshoppers, at every step. These were the ordinary ways.

Acknowledgments

Memoir is recreation of memory in a literary form. I am portraying truths of my life as clearly as I can, but I have changed some names of some individuals, and I know that others may remember these events differently. These are my memories; this is my memoir.

Thanks to Jim Redmond, who chose "Stain You Red" as first prize in the Robert Wright contest, and to Rosellen Brown, who chose it as the winner of the 2004 Speakeasy Prize for Prose, awarded by *Speakeasy* magazine, a publication of The Loft Literary Center. Thanks to Bart Schneider, editor of that magazine, for his support, too.

Ann Regan, Alison Vandenberg, and Greg Britton from Borealis Books and all the people at the press.

Before I ever proved my worth as a writer, Roger Sheffer allowed me into his already packed prose class, then agreed to be my advisor and became one of my dearest friends and best editors. Nick Healy and Tom Maltman were critical editors of several of these pieces, as well. My summertime writing group: Becky Davis, Rick Robbins, and Jeremy Johnson for their edits and their friendship; to Jer, too, for babysitting help. Thanks to Terry Davis for literary and personal advice. Thanks to Eddie Micus, my favorite author, one of my most treasured human beings, for the edits, for the craft, for the terrible history and beautiful humanity in you. Thanks to Jennifer Wendinger, my lifelong friend, for her honesty and for use of the poem, "Stained Glass." To the LeBoutilliers, thanks for opening your arms, hearts, and minds to the kids and me, as strange a situation as we are. To Chris, for our children.

To Dad. Bless you for your generosity, loyalty, and storytelling.

To my sister, Natalie Helget. Bless you for your faith.

To Mom for creativity.

To Isabella, Mitchell and Phillip. I am blessed by your existence every day.

Nate LeBoutillier. Thank you for identifying these stories, this storytelling ability in me. Thanks for the hours and hours of edits. Thanks for being a part of our lives, the kids' and mine, and for joining us on the journey, however long it is and wherever in the world it's going. You reversed the spin of my electrons.